T0311726

# Cambridge Elements ≡

Elements in Public Policy
edited by
M. Ramesh
*National University of Singapore (NUS)*
Michael Howlett
*Simon Fraser University, British Columbia*
Xun WU
*Hong Kong University of Science and Technology*
Judith Clifton
*University of Cantabria*
Eduardo Araral
*National University of Singapore (NUS)*

# GOVERNMENT TRANSPARENCY

## *State of the Art and New Perspectives*

Gregory Porumbescu
*Rutgers University, Newark*
*Yonsei University*

Albert Meijer
*Utrecht University*

Stephan Grimmelikhuijsen
*Utrecht University*

CAMBRIDGE
UNIVERSITY PRESS

# CAMBRIDGE
## UNIVERSITY PRESS

University Printing House, Cambridge CB2 8BS, United Kingdom

One Liberty Plaza, 20th Floor, New York, NY 10006, USA

477 Williamstown Road, Port Melbourne, VIC 3207, Australia

314–321, 3rd Floor, Plot 3, Splendor Forum, Jasola District Centre,
New Delhi – 110025, India

103 Penang Road, #05–06/07, Visioncrest Commercial, Singapore 238467

Cambridge University Press is part of the University of Cambridge.

It furthers the University's mission by disseminating knowledge in the pursuit of
education, learning, and research at the highest international levels of excellence.

www.cambridge.org
Information on this title: www.cambridge.org/9781108728997
DOI: 10.1017/9781108678568

© Gregory Porumbescu, Albert Meijer, and Stephan Grimmelikhuijsen 2022

First published 2022

*A catalogue record for this publication is available from the British Library.*

ISBN 978-1-108-72899-7 Paperback
ISSN 2398-4058 (online)
ISSN 2514-3565 (print)

Additional resources for this publication at www.cambridge.org/porumbescu

# Government Transparency

## State of the Art and New Perspectives

Elements in Public Policy

DOI: 10.1017/9781108678568
First published online: June 2022

Gregory Porumbescu
*Rutgers University, Newark*
*Yonsei University*

Albert Meijer
*Utrecht University*

Stephan Grimmelikhuijsen
*Utrecht University*

**Author for correspondence:** Gregory Porumbescu, greg.porumbescu
@rutgers.edu

**Abstract:** This Element argues that to understand why transparency "works" in one context but fails in another, we have to take into account how institutional (macro) and organizational (meso) contexts interact with individual behavior (micro). A review of research from each of these perspectives shows that the big promises thought to accompany greater transparency during the first two decades of the twentieth century have not been delivered. For example, transparency does not necessarily lead to better government performance and more trust in government. At the same time, transparency is still a hallmark of democratic governance, and as this Element highlights, for instance, transparency has been relatively successful in combating government corruption. Finally, by explicitly taking a multilayered perspective into account, this Element develops new paths for future research.

**Keywords:** government transparency, freedom of information, open government, public administration, good governance

ISBNs: 9781108728997 (PB), 9781108678568 (OC)
ISSNs: 2398-4058 (online), 2514-3565 (print)

# Contents

1 The Need for a Layered Understanding of Government Transparency    1

2 From Idea to Legislation and Organizational Practices    6

3 What Is Transparency?    9

4 The Macro-Level Perspective on Transparency    16

5 The Meso-Level Perspective on Transparency    27

6 The Micro-Level Perspective on Transparency    42

7 Linking and Integrating Research on Government Transparency    55

References    66

# 1 The Need for a Layered Understanding of Government Transparency

## 1.1 Election Transparency Leads to Questions about Transparency

In response to allegations of fraud and corruption during the 2020 presidential election, election administrators across the United States decided to livestream the administrative act of ballot counting on platforms such as YouTube. While this effort to make election administration more transparent was lauded as innovative, the idea itself of casting a brighter light on administrative tasks is not new – administrative transparency has been used for centuries to fight corruption, legitimize decision-making processes, and build trust.[1] Despite these efforts to increase transparency of ballot counting, a staggering 70 percent of Republicans said that they believed the 2020 presidential election was not "free and fair" (Kim 2020). It appears that the efforts to push back on claims of corruption through greater transparency fell short of winning hearts and minds.

So why did election administrators' efforts to use transparency to build confidence in the electoral system not succeed? One explanation assumes a psychological perspective on individual behavior and promotes the idea that people frequently do not believe what they see, but rather see what they believe (Epley and Gilovich 2016). For those who believe the process is corrupt, this information was never going to change their minds. A second explanation looks at organizations and focuses on the way this transparency initiative was implemented – perhaps election administrators chose to broadcast the wrong information or broadcasted the right information using the wrong technology. A third possibility pertains to the institutional level of transparency. After four years of alleging the United States' electoral system is corrupt, President Trump established a context where democratic processes were delegitimized. While the election administrators may have done their best to build trust, their efforts were doomed to fail because of persistent efforts to belittle the democratic institutions the information pertains to.

Generally, as the research discussed in this Element will show, despite transparency's strong normative appeal, its implications and antecedents are complex, layered, and context-dependent. Some have concluded that transparency has not provided better governance after all (Fenster 2015), and even when implemented meticulously and with good intentions, "transparency is not in and of itself a sufficient tool for advancing a more equitable political life" (Wood and Aronczyk 2020: 1537). In this Element, we argue that such provocative conclusions are premature and that to understand transparency's antecedents and

---

[1] In this Element, we define transparency as *the availability of information about an organization or actor allowing external actors to monitor the internal workings or performance of that organization* (Grimmelikhuijsen 2012: 55). We will discuss this definition further in Section 3.

implications, we need a contextual and layered approach to studying government transparency that combines the behavioral, organizational, and institutional perspectives discussed in the example of "failed" election transparency.

## 1.2 Why Should We Care about Transparency?

The intuition that underlines many of the purported benefits of transparency is hard to refute; individuals behave better when they know they are being watched (Holmstrom 1982); and the information transparency affords the public is critical to promoting their well-being by empowering them to make better decisions (Birkinshaw 2006). Moreover, transparency is construed as an important signal of a progressive orientation that emphasizes openness and eschews secrecy (Fenster 2017). Given the centrality of transparency to contemporary definitions of good governance, understood both in terms of values and practice, the concept has achieved "quasi-religious significance" (Hood 2006: 3). As a testament to the quasi-religious devotion to transparency, we have seen the number of Freedom of Information (FOI) Acts grow rapidly in the past two decades (Michener 2011; Kosack and Fung 2014; Figure 1 in this Element) and the establishment of international movements such as the Open Government Partnership (Piotrowski 2017), which promotes open government initiatives among national and subnational governments around the world.

There are also high-profile transparency critics who argue that the value of transparency is oversold (Etzioni 2010), or that while transparency is "an element

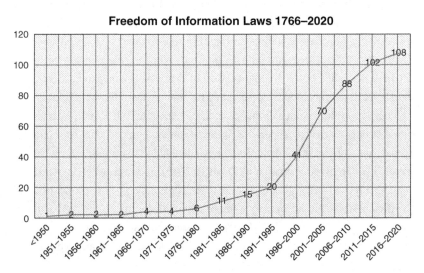

**Figure 1** Adoption of freedom of information legislation across the globe.
**Data source:** www.right2info.org/access-to-information-laws

of democracy," it comes with severe limitations and shortcomings (Schudson 2020). For example, Francis Fukuyama (2014) argues that while transparency and participation are often proposed as solutions to dysfunction, these reforms frequently make the dysfunction they sought to ameliorate worse by stifling deliberation for fear of someone saying the wrong thing. Others have argued that the instrumental and normative values of transparency are not universal (Zakaria and Yew 1994). Singaporean Prime Minister Lee Kuan Yew, who presided over Singapore during a period of tremendous economic growth in that nation and throughout much of East Asia, notes that some of the most effective anti-poverty initiatives were pursued "behind closed doors" by governments that were illiberal regimes by Western standards. Thus, while transparency may be an important path to better governance, it may not be the only path.

Even transparency optimists admit that the outcomes are not as clear and convincing as the promise of transparency suggests. Some attribute these difficulties to the impacts of transparency being "gradual, indirect, and diffuse" (Michener 2019). Another difficulty is that expectations of transparency are high, which means governments constantly seem to fail to become "fully transparent" (e.g. Fenster 2015). Thus, as Kosack and Fung (2014: 66) note, there "is a growing sense of the ambiguities in the relationship between increases in transparency and other desirable outcomes, such as greater accountability, less corruption, and improvements in basic services."

Scholars have responded in different ways to the challenges of assessing the impacts of transparency. Some focus on understanding the impact of FOI laws and whether they meaningfully impact public access to government records (Cuillier 2016). Others have advocated for new evaluation frameworks (e.g. Kosack and Fung 2014; Michener and Worthy 2018; Pozen 2019). These calls argue the importance of accounting for mechanisms responsible for lending information its impact (Michener and Bersch 2013). Instead of simply equating transparency with information availability, assessments need to view transparency reforms and the information they produce as fitting within a broader complicated social structure (Meijer et al. 2018). These efforts are important but fall short in taking the layered nature of transparency – what we referred to as the behavioral, organizational, and institutional perspectives – into account. For this reason, we believe that we need to build a comprehensive approach on the basis of the expanding literature on transparency.

## 1.3 A Layered Approach to Transparency

This Element addresses calls to develop better frameworks to understand the effects of transparency. We argue that dispelling such uncertainty requires a more coherent understanding of what transparency is. To this end, the framework we propose starts from the observation that transparency research benefits from a rich multimethod and multidisciplinary approach. This diversity has resulted in important insights into how transparency works from a behavioral (e.g. De Fine Licht et al. 2014), organizational (e.g. Flyverbom 2015), and institutional perspective (e.g. Roberts 2006; Erkkilä 2012). In this Element, we will refer to these three perspectives as the micro, meso, and macro perspectives to stress that we need to zoom in on specific interactions but also zoom out to the broader organizational and institutional settings to provide a full understanding of transparency.

While the literature on transparency is rich, it is also fragmented: certain papers focus on individual interactions at the micro level, while others highlight the organizational or institutional dimensions at the meso and macro levels. As a result, the way we think about transparency is not integrated in ways that convey a coherent big picture. At the same time, despite being disjointed, these perspectives are relevant to one another since individual interactions are shaped by organizations' and institutional settings' outcomes (Roberts 2020). For example, transparency about school performance can influence individual school choice, but to understand what information is provided, we need to understand the functioning of schools and the legal and social contexts within which the information is being disclosed.

Each perspective – the micro, meso, and macro – represents a different unit of analysis. The micro perspective focuses on individuals and their responses to transparency (Grimmelikhuijsen et al. 2017). For example, citizen decisions on how much to trust their government or which schools to send their children to. The meso perspective focuses on transparency practices of public sector organizations (Jilke et al. 2019). For example, how public organizations communicate performance information to the public. The macro perspective, which is least studied by public management and administration scholars, focuses on rules and priorities inherent to a governing context (Roberts 2020). From this point of view, the macro perspective focuses on institutions because it addresses formal and informal rules that structure the administrative work done by governments (North 1991: 97). These institutions embedded in a governing context influence the types of information organizations prioritize for disclosure and their general orientation toward openness. Given the dynamic relationship between the three perspectives, boundaries can overlap – individuals are nested in organizations, and organizations are nested in institutions. This overlap notwithstanding, understanding how these perspectives speak to one another allows us to craft a better integrated and conceptually consistent picture of government transparency (cf. Moynihan 2018).

Based on the reasons stated here, we argue that *to truly understand government transparency, we need a "layered approach" that accounts for relationships between macro-level (institutional), meso-level (organizational), and micro-level (behavioral) perspectives.* We further argue that connecting the institutional, organizational, and behavioral perspectives is essential to understanding the effects of transparency. As we will discuss at greater length later in the Element, by government transparency, we refer to one specific aspect of government – public sector administrative processes and outcomes.

To make our arguments, we expand upon an existing database of English language articles that deal with transparency and public administration (Cucciniello et al. 2017).[2] While the original database consisted of 177 articles published between 1990 and 2015, we update this database to now include 232 research articles published from 2016 to 2019, which are analyzed in terms of their contributions to micro, meso, and macro perspectives on government transparency. Details on the database, as well as the database itself, can be found in the supplementary materials. The aim of our layered approach to evaluating transparency is *to further academic understanding of how government transparency functions by developing a framework that connects research on transparency from the individual (micro), organizational (meso), and institutional (macro) levels.*

## 1.4 Outline

The balance of this Element proceeds as follows. Section 2 offers a brief overview of the philosophical foundation of transparency and how it relates to the way we understand transparency today. Section 3 offers a definition of government transparency by bringing together insights from different conceptual angles. Sections 4–6 draw on our database of published transparency research to discuss the state of the art and illustrate how research over the past few decades has investigated transparency at the micro level (Section 4), meso level (Section 5), or macro level (Section 6). Section 7 concludes the Element by outlining our layered approach, showing how insights between macro, meso,

---

[2] Delimiting the scope of this analysis is a challenge. In our analysis of the literature, we used "government transparency" as the central concept. One could argue that other concepts such as "open data," "government information," "freedom of information," "access to information," and so on, are directly related and should be included. Our argument does connect to these concepts, but we chose to keep the main focus on government transparency in the selection of literature. Thus, we engage with these streams of literature only to the extent they fall within our scope of research, so, for instance, studies that explicitly discuss how FOI legislation as a mechanism for inducing transparency are included (e.g. Worthy et al. 2017; Michener et al. 2021), but studies that do not explicitly mention transparency are not, nor are studies that focus on the transparency of other organizations such as political parties (Lindstedt and Naurin 2010).

and micro levels are interrelated, and presents recommendations for research and practice based on this layered approach.

## 2 From Idea to Legislation and Organizational Practices

While government transparency may seem like an idea only a few decades old, its intellectual roots go back much longer. To understand contemporary debates about transparency, we distinguish between three historical lines: transparency as an *idea*, transparency as *legislation*, and transparency as a *political and administrative practice*. The relation between these three lines is not unidirectional (from idea to legislation and then to political and administrative practices): changes in practices due to the introduction of new technologies have also influenced legislation and ideas about transparency. This section offers a brief historical perspective on how efforts to translate transparency as an idea and transparency in practice have interacted to shape the complex way we view transparency today.

### 2.1 Transparency as an Idea: From Debate to Performance Management

Transparency is both an old and a new concept. It is new in the sense that it is primarily used to refer to publishing government information on websites but old in the sense that the basic idea that watching others influences their behavior has been around for a long time (Hood 2006). Meijer (2009b) highlights that being able to see how things happen in person has historically played a role in societies to build trust. For instance, in traditional smaller societies, such as small towns and villages, the visibility of everyone's behavior is high and breeds interpersonal trust. Meijer (2009b: 261) stresses that transparency in traditional smaller societies was bidirectional, contextualized, and frequently informal.

The political philosopher Rousseau equated opaqueness with evil and considered transparency as the way back to the lost state of nature. Rousseau's ideas about transparency were applied to organizational settings by Jeremy Bentham. The idea that people behave better when they are being watched is central to Bentham's idea of the (1797/2001) panopticon. A panopticon is a distinct type of organization – a prison – in which all inmates are visible to the guards located in a tower in the center of the prison to ensure greater compliance with organizational rules and norms. Bentham regarded transparency as a cornerstone of government since it would prevent "conspiracy" by those who operate in the public's interest.

The ideas of Rousseau and Bentham about transparency as a governing norm guided much of the debate about transparency in the nineteenth century.

Popper (1945) renewed attention to the value of transparency with his argument that openness was needed to allow for reasonable criticism and skepticism, protect individuals, and curb power abuse of elites. Popper's ideas were widely embraced after the fall of the Nazi Empire, and openness was reaffirmed as a key value of modern democratic states.

The ideological emphasis of transparency has shifted since the 1980s. Initially, transparency was associated with progressive politics promoting trust, social justice, and bureaucratic rationality, but a different discourse has taken hold more recently: transparency to promote free choice, reduce regulation, and promote "small government" (Pozen 2018). This ideological shift aligns with many aspects of the New Public Management paradigm (Piotrowski 2007): by communicating performance and promoting choice, transparency was argued to strengthen trust in government (Hood and Heald 2006).

This brief overview shows how the way we think of transparency has evolved over time, from a feature of interpersonal relationships to a governing value to an organizational practice meant to improve individual performance and enhance public trust in government. We will now see how these ideas were translated into legislation.

## 2.2 Transparency Legislation: Mandating a Right to Access

Modern efforts to translate transparency as a value into laws that guide the actions of government organizations and individuals began in Sweden and at a time when a contemporary understanding of transparency as a hallmark of good governance was taking shape. Sweden adopted access to information legislation in 1766 during its transition from absolutist to liberal bourgeois rule (Erkkilä 2012: 6). Despite gradual steps toward transparency during the nineteenth century, Sweden remained the only country with FOI legislation until 1951, when Finland became the second country to enact such legislation. FOI legislation gained popularity after being adopted by the Johnson Administration in the United States in 1966, and this was followed by a promulgation from the 1970s onward. Roberts (2006: 15) indicates that the "transparency explosion" in the 1990s should be understood as a reaction to the fall of the Berlin Wall and the desire to repudiate the secrecy of collapsed authoritarian states. This resulted in near-exponential growth of FOI legislation across the globe in the following two decades (see Figure 1).

The rapid expansion of FOI laws seems like good news for government transparency, but there are good reasons to be more nuanced in the way we evaluate this development. Studies indicate the strength of transparency laws varies strongly (Michener 2011). Even when laws are strong on paper, there are widespread problems with strategic response behavior by governments, creating delays between information requests and responses and slow appeals systems (e.g. Hazell and Worthy 2010). In addition, governments contract out to private companies to avoid transparency regulations (Roberts 2000). Authoritarian states such as China have also adopted FOI legislation; however, Xiao (2010) found that China has adopted an FOI model in which proactive disclosure is emphasized over disclosure on demand. Moreover, the strength of this transparency law is undermined by broad exemptions and limited access.

In addition to the rise of FOI laws, the New Public Management reform agenda resulted in new forms of legislation. For example, the United States enacted the Government Performance and Results Act in 1993 (Piotrowski and Rosenbloom 2002) and the Clinger-Cohen Act in 1996 (Westerback 2000). Both acts aimed to enhance the transparency of public organizations by requiring them to provide performance information. The New Public Management reform movement influenced terms that were being used. "Publicity" and "access to information" used to be dominant terms; however, the more technical term "transparency" quickly entered political debates from the 1980s onward (Scholtes 2012).

While FOI legislation predominantly enabled access to information upon request, a new generation of legislation has been introduced that focuses on the proactive disclosure of government information (Berliner et al. 2018). President Obama issued the Open Government Directive in 2009, and this directive requires agencies to take several steps to publish timely information in accessible formats and with adequate use of new technologies (McDermott 2010). Technological advances are leading the way in this final wave of transparency legislation.

## 2.3 Transparency in Practice: From Legislation to Administration

At the core of transparency in practice is the management of government information, which traditionally means state archival work. Governments have developed archives for centuries if not millennia for internal purposes. One of the most impressive illustrations of record-keeping and archiving is *The Annals of the Joseon Dynasty* (1413 AD–1865 AD), which documents the reigns of twenty-five kings under the Joseon Dynasty, located within the Korean Peninsula. The practice of maintaining records for the internal use of autocratic governments continued from the ancient times of the Egyptians to the European monarchies of the eighteenth and nineteenth centuries until change was brought by the French revolution.

Archival practices of the monarchies in Europe were developed for internal use and had to be modified with the adoption of FOI legislation in the nineteenth and twentieth centuries to enable access by a broader and more diverse range of external users. Efforts to marry existing archival practices to FOI legislation required organizations to (1) pay careful attention to how government organizations would vet requests for information; (2) produce information from state archives in the event the public asked for it; and (3) allocate organizational resources to receive, vet, and respond to information requests. The resulting puzzle for practice was how to reconcile FOI legislation compliance with organizational performance goals. This puzzle continued throughout the eighteenth and nineteenth centuries and resulted in government organizations slowly opening up their archives and record more and more to the public (Meijer 2015).

The information revolution of the 1990s resulted in a new practice of government transparency. Today, most government agencies in democratic societies have complex structures and technologies for making their information available to citizens (Welch and Wong 2001). Indeed, through resources such as the Internet, public access to government meetings all around the world can be watched live, and even fact-checked in real time. At the same time, others have noted that these developments have made it much easier for governments to spin information disguised as transparency (Ruijer 2013). At the same time, hacking and leaking of government information have led to the direct access to government archives by external actors (Cuillier and Piotrowski 2009). Hood (2011) even highlights that this may fundamentally change the nature of transparency and gave his paper the provocative title "From FOI World to WikiLeaks World."

This historical overview in this section has identified three trends: from democratic debate to performance management; from mandating public access to government information; and from transparency legislation to transparency administration. A general pattern that can be observed across these three trends is a struggle with the value of transparency for society. Different mechanisms have been developed and relations are assumed. Our goal is to show how empirical research can help to understand these mechanisms and test assumed relations. To do so, we must first review commonly accepted definitions of transparency.

## 3 What Is Transparency?

Whereas the term "transparency" was hardly used until a few decades ago, it has become highly popular aspect of good governance (Fenster 2015). The concept of transparency purportedly lacks definitional precision and unity, making it hard to build a cumulative body of knowledge (Michener and Bersch 2013; Bauhr and Grimes 2017). In this section, we build on existing conceptualizations of transparency to provide a definition of transparency, focusing on administrative processes and outcomes, which are central to this Element. We end this section by introducing the layered – institutional, organizational, and behavioral – framework as a basis for the subsequent in-depth discussion of academic research into government transparency.

## 3.1 Defining Government Transparency

Early definitions of transparency were often broad, metaphorical, and/or normative, such as "lifting the veil of secrecy" (Davis 1998) and "the ability to look clearly through the windows of an institution" (Den Boer 1998: 105). Hood (2001: 701) defined government transparency in a somewhat narrower sense: "transparency denotes government according to fixed and published rules on the basis of information and procedures that are accessible to the public and (in some usages) within clearly demarcated fields of activity." However, Hood's definition evolved as transparency was generally conceived of as going beyond rules and procedures. Birkinshaw stated (2006: 189–191) that "transparency is the conduct of public affairs in the open or otherwise subject to public scrutiny." And Florini (2007: 5) included the consequences of viewing information in their definition of transparency as "the degree to which information is available to outsiders that enables them to have informed voice in decisions and/or to assess the decisions made by outsiders."

More recent discussions of transparency explicitly treat it as a multifaceted concept (e.g. Michener and Bersch 2013; Bauhr and Grimes 2017). At the same time the multifaceted nature sometimes leads to conflation with related concepts such as accountability, combating corruption, and open decision-making (Ball 2009). In line with calls by leading transparency scholars, we need more conceptual precision to avoid "inaccurate statements and poorly conceptualized policies." (Michener and Bersch 2013: 234).

Still, most definitions of transparency converge on the shared notion that transparency concerns the availability of information about the internal workings or performance of an organization (Cucciniello et al. 2017). Others have called this aspect of transparency "visibility," meaning that information must be reasonably complete and found with relative ease (Michener and Bersch 2013). Building on this understanding, we adopt the following definition: *Transparency is the availability of information about an organization or actor allowing external actors to monitor the internal workings or performance of that organization* (Grimmelikhuijsen 2012: 55; Grimmelikhuijsen and Meijer 2014). From this definition, we identify five distinct components of transparency: (1) availability, (2) information, (3) organization or actor, (4) external actors, and (5) internal workings.

1. *Availability.* Information availability refers to the way information is made accessible to outsiders and can refer to proactive and passive transparency. Passive transparency includes requester-type modes of transparency, such as FOI requests for government documentation. Proactive transparency means that information is routinely made available to external actors without them first having to explicitly request it. Even without the information actually being used, its public availability can influence government actions since governments change their behavior in *anticipation* of the use of information (Meijer 2000).

2. *Information.* "Information" concerns the documents, datasets, figures, recordings, and so on, made available to users, which can be used to monitor the internal workings or performance of an organization. At a basic level, information refers to data that can be used to reduce uncertainty. Michener and Bersch (2013) have referred to information quality in terms of "inferability," that is, the extent to which information can be used to draw reliable conclusions. There are various elements that increase inferability.

   a. *Granularity.* Typically, "data" are considered information in its most granular form. Think of quantitative data such as measurements of nitrogen dioxide in the air or qualitative data such as transcripts of meetings. The availability of granular information decreases the chance that information is gamed, or processed in a strategic manner (Michener and Bersch 2013). At the same time, publishing "close-to-source" data may increase concerns about privacy of individuals and raise safety or security issues (Janssen and van den Hoven 2015).

   b. *Unbiasedness.* A second element concerns the presence, or rather absence, of bias in the information. A well-known practice is that information can be spun by government officials to bring a desired narrative or conclusion to the forefront (Roberts 2005). However, even granular data can be biased when collected in a selective way (Eubanks 2018). Information bias is important because it can guide users toward wrongful inferences.

   c. *Information usability.* Instead of just divulging more information, the way information is offered to the public is also important because it influences the user's ability to understand and use the information (Mattheus and Janssen 2020). One way to achieve usability is to simplify information in such a way that it becomes understandable to a broader public (Michener and Bersch 2013). There is a tension between simplification and granularity: simplifying information might make it more usable for a broader public but comes at the cost of specificity.

3. *Organization or actor.* The third component regards the entity that discloses information. There are generally two paths to transparency: (1) an organization or actor discloses information about another organization or (2) an organization discloses information about itself. The first option occurs in various shapes. For instance, regulatory and inspection agencies increasingly tend to disclose information about supervised organizations or consumer goods (Fung et al. 2007; Van Erp 2011). A very different way in which one actor can increase (unintended) transparency of another is through whistleblowing (; Fenster 2012; Bauhr and Grimes 2017). In contrast, the second option concerns governments that publish information about their own decisions or actions. Such forms of transparency can be pursued through television broadcasting, newspaper announcements, or by publishing information on official websites. For instance, local governments publish decision-making procedures, meeting minutes, and videos online.

4. *External actors.* External actors are stakeholders (groups or individuals) who are the intended recipients of information. It is important to explicate these external actors because without specifying these stakeholders we fail to consider that "information may be accessible to, for example, initiated experts but impenetrable to a lay audience" (Bauhr and Grimes 2017). Oftentimes, citizens do not access government information directly, but rather through third parties, sometimes called "infomediaries" such as journalists, civil society organizations (CSOs), or experts. Typically, individual journalists use FOI legislation to force governments to provide sensitive information and they often play an active role in making the information usable for the broader public (Van Zyl 2014). This does not mean citizens only depend on infomediaries. Citizens, for example, consult government websites to learn about opportunities to participate in local decision-making processes, such as town hall meetings on local issues, or they monitor the performance of public services to call governments to account.

*Internal workings.* Here we discuss the "internal workings" of government organizations that can be made transparent. One way of looking at these internal workings is to apply them to a set of *activities* that governments perform (Heald 2006). Grimmelikhuijsen and Welch (2012) developed a framework that consists of three broad activities to evaluate government transparency: (1) transparency of decision-making processes, (2) transparency of policy content, and (3) transparency of policy outcomes or effects. A second framework was developed by Cucciniello and Nasi (2014) who delineated forms of transparency according to the area of government as they set out three widely investigated objects of transparency: (1) financial or budget transparency, (2) administrative transparency, and (3) political transparency. Budget transparency refers to information about the financial situation of a government and outlines how public actors use the financial resources they are allocated (building on Pina et al. 2010). Administrative transparency is the disclosure of information from the administration or bureaucracy pertaining to the activities of public organizations, missions, and operations (Cucciniello et al. 2017). Finally, political transparency relates to the openness of elected bodies such as parliaments or local councils and refers to information pertaining to political representatives (Cucciniello et al. 2012).

At its core, our definition presents an information relation between two actors. As Meijer (2013: 429) explains, "Government transparency is constructed through complex interactions between a variety of political and social actors, within sets of formal and informal rules, and the availability of constantly evolving technologies." To develop a further understanding of the various antecedents, mechanisms, and outcomes of transparency, we need to delve into the nature of the relation between the monitoring actor and the monitored actor. We will do this by arguing that this relation needs to be studied at three levels: individual, organizational, and institutional.

## 3.2 Transparency as an Institutional, Organizational, and Individual Field of Study

Generic approaches to analyzing government transparency, such as counting the speed of responses to FOI requests, are flawed in that they constitute a reductionist approach to understanding a complex social phenomenon (Michener 2019). These efforts run the risk of reducing transparency into an exercise in box ticking (Hood 2010: 992). Pozen (2019) argues the importance of taking a "sociological turn" when analyzing transparency, which is better able to capture the social construction of transparency and its subsequent broad effects. Michener (2019: 136) argues that an emphasis on measurement results in an inaccurate understanding of the effects of transparency, which are "gradual, indirect, and diffuse." This debate thus brings into focus the tension mentioned earlier between efforts to construct general definitions of transparency on the one hand and, on the other hand, the distinctive institutional, organizational, and individual dynamics of transparency. The approach we take to resolving this tension is to develop a layered approach to analyzing transparency. This layered approach enables researchers to capture institutional, organizational, and individual dynamics and, as a result will not only position us to better understand what transparency is, but also what it does.

### Institutions and the Macro Level

Studies at the macro level focus on institutional contributions to transparency. This is the oldest line of empirical research in this field and early work mainly focuses on the dissemination of FOI legislation. For instance, Alasdair Roberts' (2006) "Blacked Out: Government Secrecy in the Information Age" and Tero Erkkilä's (2012) "Government Transparency: Impacts and Unintended Consequences" provide a broad overview of the way in which FOI legislation has been enacted worldwide. They also critically analyze to what extent secrecy in government is protected despite this legislation and what the impacts and unintended consequences are. More recently, the macro perspective has also been applied to studying the role of institutions in open data. Safarov (2019) analyzes the institutional differences between the Netherlands, Sweden, and the United Kingdom to identify institutional differences and uses these to explain variations in openness. Finally, the institutional perspective is not limited to cross-country comparisons. Macro analyses also focus on the role of institutions at a regional or local level in government transparency.

### Organizations and the Meso Level

Studies at the meso level focus on the organizational implementation of government transparency. These studies draw from sociology theory to understand transparency as an organizational practice. This line of research consists of a limited number of older studies looking into the organizational implementation of FOI legislation and a greater number of more recent studies focusing on open data and tools such as social media. In his study of the "complex dynamics of transparency," Meijer (2013), for example, shows how government organizations develop public disclosure practices in response to pressure from external stakeholders. From this perspective, efforts to manage government transparency are strategic and play to the political interests of the organization disseminating the information. Albu and Flyverbom (2019) critically examine organizational transparency and, in line with Meijer (2013), argue that transparency is not merely about information quality but is also "performative": it brings out strategic and political considerations.

### Individuals and the Micro Level

Micro-level research, the most recent addition to the study of transparency, is conducted at the individual level and focuses on individual "cognitions,

**Table 1** Perspectives on studying government transparency

| Level | Focus |
|-------|-------|
| Macro | Formal and informal institutions interacting with government transparency |
| Meso | Organizational and managerial practices interacting with government transparency |
| Micro | Perceptions, attitudes, and behavioral responses of individual civil servants and citizens interacting with government transparency |

attributes, and behaviors of various kinds" (Jilke et al. 2019: 246–247). This research often uses theories and methods from psychology to understand how transparency is enacted by civil servants and how transparency influences the attitudes and cognitions of citizens. For example, in his study "Transparency and trust. An experimental study of online disclosure and trust in government," Grimmelikhuijsen (2012) presents a series of experiments that he conducted to develop a nuanced and in-depth understanding of the effects of transparency on citizen trust. Similarly, in her study "Policy area as a potential moderator of transparency effects: An experiment," de Fine Licht (2014) shows how the relation between transparency and trust is mediated by the policy area. Porumbescu et al. (2017) focused their study on the relation between transparency and policy support and shows that there is no one-on-one relation between transparency, understanding, and support. A recent addition to the studies at the micro level focuses on the impact of transparency not on citizens, but on civil servants. De Boer (2020) conducted a series of experiments to establish causal relations between transparency and the perceived relational distance between government inspectors and their inspectees.

## *A Layered Framework for Studying Government Transparency*

An overview of the different perspectives on studying transparency is presented in Table 1:

This overview of the different perspectives highlights how the study of transparency has evolved from an emphasis on FOI and a political science and legal perspective to a multidisciplinary field that aims to provide an understanding of political and administrative transparency practices from a macro (political system), meso (organizational practice), and micro (behavior and cognition) perspectives.

Scholars studying government transparency tend to look at transparency through a single lens, but one should notice that some studies do combine the different lenses, often implicitly. A first example is provided by Bauhr and Grimes (2014) who analyzed individual responses taken from multilevel data from the World Values Survey (micro level) and compared these responses across countries with low and high levels of reported corruption (macro level). A second example is an analysis of transparency in the Council of the European Union by Hillebrandt (2017) where he shows how institutional changes in transparency legislation and Council politics (macro level) have resulted in diverging organizational practices in specific EU-related administrative bodies (meso level). These two examples underscore the central argument in this Element: we need to combine the three lenses to develop a thorough and more complete understanding of government transparency. We need to understand the institutional dynamics, organizational practices, individual responses, and how they interact.

A sophisticated understanding of a social phenomenon, such as government transparency requires that we not only zoom in on the micro level to understand the individual civil servants and citizens but also zoom out to the macro context to understand how these individuals are influenced by organizational environments and transparency rules. The theoretical perspective that we developed in this section can help us to organize the rich literature on government transparency and to draw conclusions about what we know about the different levels. In the next three sections, we review research related to each of these lenses.

## 4 The Macro-Level Perspective on Transparency

### 4.1 Introducing the Macro-Level Perspective on Transparency

The institutional perspective adopted in this Element focuses on transparency as a construct that shapes the state's governance efforts. Institutions represent "informal constraints, such as sanctions, taboos, customs, traditions, and codes of conduct," and "formal rules such as constitutions, laws, property rights," which have been established to "create order and reduce uncertainty in exchange" (North 1991: 97). From the institutional perspective, transparency functions as a necessary condition for other prominent qualities of a governing context, such as corruption, trust in government, and government performance (Jilke et al. 2019).

Information flows pertaining to government processes and outcomes are an important feature of institutions. These flows play a fundamental role in communicating rules, delineating focal actors, and shaping exchanges between them (Berliner and Erlich 2015). Heald (2006) explains that information flows establish a basis for accountability by facilitating *monitoring* of government actions and promoting the idea of "answerability" (Bovens 2010). New Public Management reforms have promoted routine proactive disclosure of performance information to make governments more accountable to the public (Pollitt and Bouckaert 2004). Here, the objective is not solely to facilitate sanctioning or rewarding government for its performance, but also, from a broad perspective on accountability, to inform the public about what their government is doing.

Information flows can also be structured to cultivate *collaboration*. For example, in open government initiatives, governments publicly disclose data and other relevant government information to fuel collaboration and civic engagement (Wilson and Chakraborty 2019). Rather than using public disclosure to emphasize answerability, the emphasis is placed on communicating opportunities for the public to engage with government to co-produce public value (Porumbescu et al. 2020). This might mean public health departments publish health data on influenza prevalence to encourage flu vaccinations, whereas cities may use mobile applications to manage congestion or pollution.

This institutional perspective on transparency dovetails with discussions on the role public organizations play in realizing different good governance objectives, such as improved performance, trust in government, and low corruption (Weiss 2000; Dahl 2008; Holmberg et al. 2009). In these discussions, monitoring-oriented information flows are highlighted as an institutional feature that promotes accountability, whereas collaboration-oriented information flows engender civic engagement (Hood and Heald 2006). One implication of this perspective is that institutional transparency is not necessarily a harbinger of democratic behavior. Specifically, nondemocratic institutions can use monitoring and collaboration-oriented information flows to encourage a narrower range of apolitical accountability and collaboration to improve the quality of government. For example, research on access to information laws shows that considerable variation exists in terms of how these laws function in democratic as opposed to more authoritarian regimes (Relly and Cuillier 2010). In this way, we observe democratic and authoritarian regimes promoting transparency, albeit in different ways.

In this section, we will discuss literature that presents an institutional perspective on transparency systematically by focusing on the definition of transparency, the focus in the research on either antecedents or implications, the way transparency is measured, and finally, the main substantive themes. Table 2 presents an overview of the issues and questions that will be addressed in this section.

## 4.2 How Is Transparency Measured from a Macro-Level Perspective?

A key finding in our analysis of the literature is that macro-level transparency is measured in very different ways, which means that we need to be very careful in aggregating results of research. Of the 109 articles that examine transparency at

**Table 2** Summary of literature review macro-level perspective on transparency

| | |
|---|---|
| Summary | 132 articles published between 1990 and 2019 |
| Definition of macro-level perspective | The macro perspective views government transparency as an effort to distill a particular governing order by prioritizing information flows targeting collaboration with and monitoring by external actors. |
| How transparency is studied | Antecedents of transparency (109)<br>Implications of transparency (23) |
| How is transparency measured | • Financial information (35)<br>• ICT (28)<br>• Legislation (27)<br>• Index (20)<br>• Open government (4)<br>• Perceptual (4)<br>• Sustainability/environmental information (6)<br>• Transparency reforms (8) |
| Main substantive themes | Antecedents<br>• Technology (17)<br>• Financial and political pressure (30)<br>• Context (62)<br>Implications<br>• Economic implications (7)<br>• Good governance (14)<br>• Public opinion (2) |

the macro level, the majority (35) evaluate transparency as a *financial construct*. For example, De Renzio and Masud (2011) examine key budget information published by national governments to create an open budget index. Deng et al. (2013) examine online disclosure of local government budgets in China. One explanation for the strong emphasis on transparency as a financial construct relates to concerns over corruption as well as the fact that financial transparency is easy to measure because this information tends to be quantitative.

The next most common approach to studying transparency is *Internet-based disclosure* of government information (28). One common approach is to analyze the amount of information governments post online, as Royo et al. (2014) do. Others add more nuance, examining not only the amount of information, but also the types of information. For example, Grimmelikhuijsen and Welch (2012)'s measures of ICT-based transparency focus not only on quantity but also on the types of information disclosed online.

Twenty-seven articles measure transparency as a *legislative construct*. For example, Dragos et al. (2012) study the implementation of procedural transparency requirements in Romania. Similarly, Roberts studies FOIA implementation in the United Kingdom. Others examine compliance with FOIA legislation (2005). Lagunes and Pocasangre (2019) conducted a field experiment in Mexico to test responsiveness to FOI requests. Worthy et al. (2017), also using a field experiment, studied whether legally mandated requests for information worked better at accessing government information than informal asks.

The remaining articles present a variety of measures. We found papers focusing on comprehensive indices to measure transparency (20), open government (4), public perceptions of government transparency (4), the amount of sustainability/environmental information posted to government websites (6), or qualitative features of transparency reforms (8).

Overall, a first takeaway is that measures of transparency at the macro level tend to focus on financial information. Part of the reason for this may be substantive, related to the importance of financial information for accountability and reducing corruption, but there may also be pragmatic reasons for this emphasis in research – this information is easier for researchers to incorporate into empirical research designs because of its quantitative nature. A second key takeaway is the relative infrequent use of indices to measure transparency. Transparency is a complex and multifaceted construct, but this richness is often lost in empirical research. A final key point to consider is the lack of measurement equivalence in transparency research. Since studies rely on different ways of operationalizing transparency, one should be very careful in aggregating findings of different studies.

## 4.3 Transparency as a Dependent Variable from a Macro-Level Perspective

Of the 132 articles that empirically examine institutional transparency, 109 of them focus on determinants, which can be divided into three groups: *technology*, *pressure*, and *context*. By analyzing determinants of transparency, we seek to understand how technology, pressure, and context influence monitoring- and collaboration-oriented information flows. We review each group of determinants in turn.

### Technology

Roughly 13 percent ($n = 17$) of empirical articles on institutional transparency focus on technology as a determinant of institutional transparency. The overall argument is that, at the institutional level, the adoption of technology by governments alters the priorities of public disclosure (Searson and Johnson 2010). Technology and, in particular, the Internet allow governments to directly disseminate information to the general public, instead of relying on third parties, or information mediaries.

Seven of the articles focus on the use of technology for facilitating collaboration-oriented information flows. The potential of technology to foster more transparent, collaborative, and participatory relationships between governments and the public is central to prominent reform initiatives such as the open government movement (McDermott 2010). Yet findings from this strand of literature are mixed. For example, Gandia et al. (2016) examine the use of social media by Spanish local governments and their findings suggest that there is no apparent commitment to meaningfully increasing public engagement. On the other hand, Song and Lee (2016) also consider the role of technology in enhancing collaboration-oriented information flows and show that government use of social media to publicly disseminate information can establish a foundation for collaboration.

The remaining ten articles discuss government use of technology as a tool for increasing monitoring-oriented forms of transparency. For example, Stewart and Davis (2016) argue for a structural overhaul of FOIA legislation that "takes advantage of modern record-keeping technologies." Bolívar et al. (2015), however, show that the use of technology for purposes of public disclosure varies according to administrative culture and country. A final key theme from this work is that governments are consistently more successful in using technology to stimulate monitoring-oriented information flows when compared to cooperation-oriented information flows.

### Financial and Political Pressure

The second class of determinants speaks to the impact of financial and political pressure on information flows. In delineating focal actors and information priorities, financial and political pressure play a critical role in shaping the balance that is struck between monitoring and collaborative information flows. Roughly 28 percent ($n = 30$) of the empirical articles examining the determinants of institutional transparency focus on pressure; eleven deal with financial pressure, eighteen address political pressure, and one examines both political and financial pressure.

Among the studies focusing exclusively on financial pressure, a general pattern is that economic downturns tend to stimulate greater transparency. For example, Arapis and Reitano (2018) draw on data from fifty-nine countries from 2006 to 2012 to demonstrate a positive association between economic recessions and levels of fiscal transparency. Brusca et al. (2016) show that in Italian and Spanish municipalities there is a positive association between austerity measures and levels of disclosure. Part of the reason why economic downturn drives greater disclosure is because increased levels of transparency lower the cost of debt. That is, in economic downturns, governments may need to borrow financial capital and, to keep the costs down or as a condition of the loan (Abushamsieh et al. 2014), increase levels of (financial) disclosure.

With respect to political pressure, diversity in representation, especially as it relates to gender, is frequently highlighted. For example, Araujo and Tejedo-Romero (2018) show that greater gender parity in terms of political representation in Spanish municipalities was associated with greater transparency. The salience of political competition is also noted. Berliner (2014) uses data from a range of national settings to demonstrate that political competition shows that FOI legislation passage is more common in settings where "opposition parties pose more credible challenges to incumbents and when recent turnover in executive office has been frequent" (479). The argument is that parties who believe there is a chance they will be voted out of office use FOI legislation as a tool for ensuring continued access to government information (see also Alt et al. 2006; Esteller-More and Otero 2012). In addition to diversity of representation and political competition, the ideological orientation of a government also plays a role in shaping levels of transparency. Grimmelikhuijsen and Welch (2012) show that left-leaning local councils tend to be more transparent local governments. On the other hand, Garrido-Rodriguez et al. (2017) show that conservative governments tend to place a stronger emphasis on transparency. One way of interpreting these conflicting results is that the influence of ideology on support for transparency is context-specific. As intimated by the discussion earlier, both political pressure and financial pressure place a strong emphasis on monitoring-oriented information flows.

## Context

The final set of determinants relates to context. Forty-six percent ($n = 62$) of articles in our database examine different qualities of context as a determinate of institutional transparency. Following Jilke et al. (2019: 248), we take context to mean structural features that characterize the environment an institution exists in, which include values, culture, and legal traditions. Context differs from technology, as well as financial and political pressure because these sources of influence on institutional transparency can be global in nature. Therefore, institutional context is important to consider when attempting to understand why the balance between monitoring and collaborative information flows, and thus institutional transparency differs across settings.

Firstly, culture is a quality of institutional context that receives attention. Navarro-Galera et al. (2017) find that Nordic countries are less active in disclosing information related to sustainability policies when compared to Anglo-Saxon countries. Ríos et al. (2013) use a sample of ninety-three countries to demonstrate that administrative culture helps to explain levels of budget disclosure among central governments. Part of the effect of culture could be driven by power differentials; the more hierarchically power is diffused within an administrative context, the lower the levels of transparency (Bolívar et al. 2015). This is because opening up a hierarchy can facilitate changes that threaten to diffuse power held by those at the top. This point is perhaps best illustrated in authoritarian contexts, such as China. Documenting China's first nationwide open government information regulations (OGIR) implemented in 2007, Liu (2016) argues that China's OGIR is similar to the US FOIA in its emphasis on transparency and accountability but differs in that information flows in China are geared toward strengthening internal accountability mechanisms, such as judicial review.

A second strand of inquiry examines how contextual features moderate the implementation of transparency legislation. David-Barrett and Okamura (2016) observe that transparency initiatives are often adopted and implemented in contexts with high levels of corruption to signal a credible commitment to anti-corruption reform to the international community. On the other hand, Dragos et al. (2012) highlight issues in implementing transparency legislation in Romanian local governments, noting issues ranging from administrative capacity to cultural and social characteristics of the communities these reforms are being implemented in. Taking stock of challenges context poses for government compliance with FOI legislation, Worthy et al. (2017) show that FOI legislation is more effective at ensuring public access to government information than informal requests. Thus, an initial conclusion is that while evidence indicates qualities of an institutional context can pose challenges for implementing legislation intending to enhance transparency, these laws still provide an important baseline for information access.

In summary, empirical research on transparency uncovers three sets of determinants related to technology, pressure, and context. This is illustrated in Figure 2. While the use of technology by governments to increase transparency is often argued to place a greater emphasis upon collaboration-oriented information flows that encourage outcomes such as civic engagement and participation in administrative decision-making processes and public service delivery,

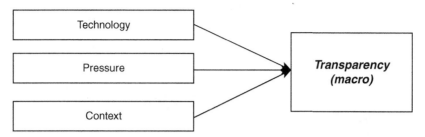

**Figure 2** Antecedents of macro-level transparency

evidence indicates that governments primarily use technology for purposes of enhancing monitoring-oriented information flows. In this regard, all three sets of determinants are similar in their effects on institutional transparency in that they prioritize monitoring-oriented information flows.

## 4.4 Transparency as an Independent Variable from a Macro-Level Perspective

Only 18 percent ($n = 23$) of empirical research articles in our database dealing with institutional transparency focus on implications. Implications of institutional transparency can be grouped into three categories – economic, quality of government, and public attitudes. Each class of implications is elaborated upon in the following text. A summary of implications can be found in Figure 3.

### *Economic Implications*

Five percent ($n = 7$) of articles focus on economic implications of institutional transparency. From an institutional perspective, transparency can improve economic outcomes by improving the quality of information decision-makers have access to, thereby reducing uncertainty that accompanies financial transactions. This point figures prominently in work by Gavazza and Lizzeri (2009), who show that transparency of government spending leads to "more efficient financing of any exogenously fixed amount of transfer spending." Similarly, Bastida et al. (2017) explain that higher levels of transparency are associated with lower costs of sovereign debt because transparency "reduces information asymmetries between governments and financial markets, which, in turn diminishes the spread requested by investors" (106). However, Copelovitch et al. (2018) note that these effects might be conditional upon context – namely levels of preexisting public indebtedness. That is, the relationship between transparency and sovereign borrowing costs is stronger in countries that have low levels of debt.

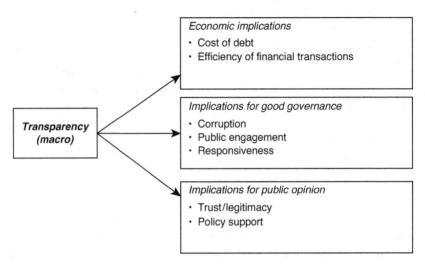

**Figure 3** Implications of macro-level transparency

## Good Governance

Implications of institutional transparency for good governance are widely discussed and relate to a range of outcomes, such as responsiveness, public engagement, and corruption. In our database, 11 percent (*n* = 14) address different aspects of good governance.

With respect to corruption, Bauhr et al. (2020) assess implications of institutional transparency through a lens of public procurement. Their findings indicate that being more explicit in calls for proposals "establishes conditions for fair competition and prevents corruption by allowing firms to monitor the requirements and the formal processes for selection of the winning bid." One reason for this is that clarifying criteria in terms of who is allowed to bid and the evaluation process make it difficult for the government to stack the deck in favor of a preselected bidder. Taking a slightly different perspective on corruption, Bauhr and Grimes (2014) examine the implications of institutional transparency for civic engagement in contexts where levels of corruption are high. The authors show that in settings where corruption is endemic, increased transparency leads to resignation and demobilizes the public. This study qualifies our understanding of when greater transparency leads to greater accountability, demonstrating that this may be true, but only to the extent that the public feels efforts to hold government accountable will make a difference.

Building upon the relationship between access to government information, mobilization, and perceptions of self-efficacy, Yavuz and Welch (2014) show that greater website openness is associated with greater perceived usefulness of technology and higher levels of public participation in administrative decision-making processes. Yet the authors also note an important condition in their discussion – this correlation is contingent upon context.

## Public Opinion

About 1.5 percent ($n = 2$) of studies in our database explore the implications of institutional transparency for public opinion. Conventional wisdom posits that more open institutions benefit from stronger relationships with the public than more closed institutions. The reasoning is that open institutions signal they have nothing to hide when interacting with the public and no ulterior motives when drafting and implementing governing strategies. As a result, the public operates from a more positive baseline when evaluating government and its policies.

Arellano-Gault (2016) argues that we need to think carefully about the contours of the relationship between institutional transparency and trust in government (see also Roelofs 2019). He analyzes transparency reforms inspired by New Institutional Economics undertaken in Mexico in the early 2000s. Among other things, these reforms intended to build trust in government. However, Arellano-Gault argues that the logic underpinning these reforms is too reductionist, failing to account for the complex social and political dynamics that characterize the public sector. Adding further nuance to our understanding of the implications of institutional transparency for public opinion, Chen and Cho (2019) examine the impact of monitoring-oriented and collaboration-oriented information flows on policy support. Interestingly, the authors find that monitoring-oriented information flows are more effective at increasing policy support when compared to collaboration-oriented information flows. The authors explain this is because more interactive communication inherent to collaboration-oriented information flows is perceived as marketing and therefore less credible than monitoring-oriented information flows, which are more passive in the way they communicate policy information to the public. Put differently, the public may see monitoring information flows as being more objective and therefore credible than collaboration-oriented information flows.

## 4.5 Main Findings

Three conclusions are taken from this review of the large body of empirical research on institutional transparency.

### An Emphasis on Determinants

Our overview highlights that most of the research at the macro-level focuses on determinants of institutional transparency – what makes government more transparent? – while far fewer articles have examined the effects of institutional transparency – what does government transparency bring? This emphasis on finding ways to make institutions more transparent, before deriving a careful understanding of just what transparency at this level can accomplish, seems to be related to many positive assumptions about transparency. That is, efforts to improve institutional transparency, in any form, are assumed to be desirable and research into the effects of transparency is generally not regarded as a priority.

### An Emphasis on Good Governance

A second notable trend is that efforts to evaluate the impacts of institutional transparency emphasize implications for different aspects of good governance, such as low corruption or government performance and, to a much lesser extent, address implications for public opinion, such as trust in government. Despite its diffuse impact on a governing context, studies tend to view institutional transparency as contributing toward a limited range of outcomes, with little consideration for impacts on individual citizens. Thus, the conclusion here is that extant approaches to evaluating the effects of institutional transparency may contribute to a systemic understanding of what transparency at this level is good for rather than having a focus on people's perceptions.

### Inattention to Measurement

A final observation taken from the empirical research on institutional transparency is the inattention to questions of how to measure transparency at this level. As the literature highlights, measuring transparency is challenging because of the many, interconnected aspects of this concept. The often-used solution to this issue is to evaluate transparency in terms of a single dimension, such as the availability of government information. While offering a starting point to evaluate the effects of transparency, this narrow evaluation approach ends up discounting the breadth of the concept of institutional transparency. Thus, the conclusion is that, just as with the way we evaluate the effects of transparency, our inattention to the way we measure institutional transparency may also limit our understanding of the value that transparency at this level creates.

## 4.6 Research Directions

### A More Critical Perspective on Institutional Transparency

While empirical research on institutional transparency tends to focus on the potential positive implications of transparency, a robust understanding necessitates more critical assessments of transparency at this level. An important step in this direction is to focus attention toward a richer assessment of potential outcomes of institutional transparency. Not only empirical assessments but also conceptual work that theorizes the broader events that efforts to implement greater institutional transparency put into place. One area in particular that deserves attention in this regard relates to equity. Knowledge is said to be the great equalizer, but institutional transparency may actually strengthen the given social status quo.

### How Do We Measure Transparency as a Value?

Inevitably, a better understanding of institutional transparency will require strategies to account for the complexity of transparency at this level of analysis. While extant approaches focus on access to or disclosure of information, what is missing is an effort to account for the value dimensions of institutional transparency. One key step toward addressing this issue at the institutional level is for research to spend more time conceptualizing the value proposition of transparency and how that differs and relates to complementary public values. While our Element provides preliminary insights on the importance of doing so, additional work on this topic is needed to eventually develop a richer operationalization of institutional transparency in the form of a measurement model.

## 5 The Meso-Level Perspective on Transparency

### 5.1 Introducing the Meso-Level Perspective on Transparency

The meso level directs our attention to how transparency is shaped in and by organizations. The meso level focuses on the manifestations, antecedents, and implications of organizational policies and managerial practices (Albu and Flyverbom 2019). The key assumption in this approach is that the public sector consists of public organizations and, for this reason, government transparency needs to be understood as the result of organizational actions.

An example of the meso perspective on transparency – the focus on the transparency of organizations – is the work by Ruijer et al. (2020) on the politics of open government data. They study the specific reactions of a province in the Netherlands and a municipality in France to understand how these specific organizations translate national legislative frameworks for transparency into specific organizational actions of making datasets available to citizens and stakeholders. The objective of the research is to understand patterns in organizational responses to institutional pressures for transparency.

The ambition at this level is to develop an understanding of how organizations produce – or do not produce – transparency. Transparency is thus not understood merely as the result of legislation or political dynamics at the macro level, but rather of a set of organizational practices (Albu and Flyverbom 2019). Building upon the social theory of organizations (Bolman and Deal 2017; Scott and Falcone 1998), organizational structure, culture, procedures, competencies, and funding along with external structures such as interorganizational networks and institutional frameworks are typically studied to understand how and why organizations realize transparency.

In terms of the number of publications, this level takes the middle ground between the micro and the macro: it is more researched than the micro level but less than the macro level. In our dataset covering publications over the period 1990–2019, we found fifty-four publications focusing primarily or partly on government transparency at the meso level. An overview of these publications is presented in Table 3. In this section, we provide an overview of how transparency is measured (Section 5.2), as well as what kind of antecedents (Section 5.3) and implications (Section 5.4) of transparency are identified at the meso level. In Section 5.5, we summarize the main findings from this level and we finalize the section by formulating some research directions (Section 5.6).

## 5.2 How Is Transparency Measured at the Meso Level?

Similar to many concepts in the study of public administration, meso-level transparency is conceptualized and measured in different manners. Some authors explicitly notice that transparency is difficult to measure (Bauhr and Grimes 2017; Ingrams 2018). Heimstädt and Dobusch (2018) explicitly state: "Transparency is in vogue, yet it is often used as an umbrella concept for a wide array of phenomena." This section presents an overview of the various approaches to measuring transparency that we found in the literature.

### Broad measures of transparency

There is no unified or coherent measure of transparency at the meso level. In some approaches, fiscal indicators take precedence, and indicators such as multiyear expenditure forecast, annual budget cycles, and performance information reporting are combined (e.g. Alt et al. 2002). Michael and Bates (2003) also present broad measures of fiscal and monetary transparency, which focus on (1) clarity of roles, responsibilities, and objectives; (2) public availability of information; (3) open budget preparation, execution, and reporting; and (4) accountability and assurance of integrity. Another broad approach is presented by Ganapati and Reddick (2012, 2014). They have a multifactorial manner of

**Table 3** Summary of the literature review of the meso-level perspective on transparency

| | |
| --- | --- |
| Summary | Fifty-four articles were published between 1990 and 2019 |
| Definition of meso-level perspective | The meso-level perspective on transparency studies the implications and antecedents of government transparency from the point of view of organization in their institutional and stakeholder environment. |
| How is transparency studied? | Dependent variable (29)<br>Independent variable (14)<br>Both independent and dependent variable (5)<br>Developing measures for transparency (6) |
| How is transparency measured? (greater than or equal to three studies) | • Government websites (29)<br>• Broad measures of transparency (5)<br>• Transparency initiatives and policies (4)<br>• Social media (4)<br>• Disclosure on request (4)<br>• Compliance with obligations (4)<br>• Proactive reporting (3) |
| Main substantive themes (greater than or equal to three studies) | Antecedents<br>• Management interventions (10)<br>• Technology (7)<br>• Actions of organizational actors (5)<br>• Stakeholder environment (4)<br>Implications<br>• Implications for the organization (3): for example, (risk) management, financial decisions<br>• Implications for relations between stakeholders and organization (9): for example, trust/legitimacy, accountability, participation corruption |

measuring e-transparency with different items, such as an established implementation plan, committee for overseeing open e-government implementation, and having an established mechanism for assessing the quality of online information. These examples show there is such a diversity of organizational contexts that authors develop measures tailored to their specific study. While this is not a criticism of these studies it does make study outcomes harder to compare findings.

## Government websites

A popular way to measure transparency is by analyzing government websites. While most studies analyze the website of a specific organization, certain studies focus on collaborative data platforms (e.g. Chen and Chang 2020). Many studies focus on online transparency regarding a specific topic. Ortiz-Rodríguez et al. (2018) focus on online transparency regarding the sustainability of public policies, D'onza et al. (2017) focus on disclosure of anti-corruption measures, Ruijer et al. (2020) focus specifically on earthquakes and transport, and Meijer (2005) analyzes risk maps. Again, a relatively large part of scholarly attention is paid to financial transparency (Caba Pérez et al. 2005; Justice et al. 2006; Bolívar et al. 2007; Bolívar et al. 2013; Thornton and Thornton 2013; Worthy 2015; Rauh 2016). A sophisticated method for studying online transparency is presented by Szabo et al. (2016) who follows Grimmelikhuijsen (2012) and Cucciniello and Nasi (2014) by presenting a multifaceted conceptualization stressing both different types of transparency (e.g. institutional transparency, policy transparency) and different dimensions (completeness, color, and comprehensibility).

## Transparency initiatives and policies

Some authors do not measure transparency directly but focus on transparency or open government initiatives. Ingrams (2018), for example, evaluates transparency initiatives on indicators such as potential impact, effectiveness, and goal clarity. Puron-Cid (2014) investigates the open government initiative to understand the possible enablers and inhibitors that public officials face during the adoption of this type of project. Ito (2002) investigates how prefectures in Japan adopt transparency policies since they are interested in the dissemination of transparency as a policy idea. Finally, Bertot et al. (2014) examine the ways in which the current information policy framework addresses policy challenges related to open data requirements. It should be noted that in all these studies, the initiatives and policies are a proxy for transparency, and transparency is not measured directly.

## Social media

Digital transparency efforts make up an important part of the corpus. Not only websites but also social media channels are studied by various scholars. For instance, Avery and Graham (2013) analyze how social media are used as a strategic and public relations function to promote a more participatory and transparent government. Gunawong (2015) explores social media's contribution to transparency by Thailand's public sector. Bonson et al. (2012) assess the use of social media tools for generating transparency in EU local governments. Bertot et al. (2012) also look at social media and they specifically analyze the relations between transparency through social media and through government websites.

## Compliance with obligations

Some investigations check whether government organizations comply with legal obligations or best practice codes. Larbi et al. (2019) analyzed whether Colleges of Education (COEs) in Ghana comply with transparency provisions in the Public Procurement Act. Kimball (2011) conduct a legal statutory analysis to investigate whether US states have enacted open government provisions. Garde Sanchez et al. (2014) investigate whether Supreme Audit Institutions in Spain comply with best practice codes of transparency and accountability. Caamaño-Alegre et al. (2013) measure whether fiscal transparency in Spanish local governments matches the international Code of Good Practices on Fiscal Transparency.

## Disclosure on request

Next to the information availability, transparency can be created on request. Some meso-level-oriented studies focus on this type of transparency. For instance, Ruijer (2017) studied the role of government communication offices in responses to requests for government information in the United States and the Netherlands. Arya and Sharma (2014) look at responses to Right to Information (RTI) applications and citizens' efforts to exercise their right to demand information about the delivery of entitlements in Rajasthan (India). In addition, Meijer (2003) investigates the responses of organizations to requests for information by various external institutions (e.g. the Court of Audit, Ombudsman). In a later study, Meijer and colleagues similarly looked at organizational responses to data requests from citizens (Meijer et al. 2014).

## Proactive reporting

Even though reports are generally available through websites, we recognize proactive reporting as a separate form. Caba Pérez et al. (2009) specifically analyze governmental financial reports to check whether they include financial information of sufficient quality to support decision-making by different users and present financial information that is comparable to the information of other public sector bodies. Alcaraz-Quiles et al. (2014, 2015) evaluate sustainability reporting in the public sector in Spain.

### Open meetings

Another classic form of transparency that is hardly investigated is open meetings, such as town hall meetings where ordinary citizens can come and comment on decision-making processes. Again, we only found one study: Piotrowski and Borry (2010) focus on open meetings in their study of all American states.

Overall, *measuring* transparency is highly varied and context-specific. Some broad measures have been applied but most of these turned out to be contextual and tailored to specific forms of transparency. Surprisingly few studies analyzed more conventional forms of transparency such as passive disclosure and open meetings. Instead, the scholarly effort seems to focus on digital transparency such as government websites, mandatory reporting, and social media.

## 5.3 What Are the Antecedents of Meso-Level Transparency?

In total, we identified twenty-nine studies that examined the antecedents of meso-level transparency and in addition we found five articles that studied transparency both as a dependent and independent variable.[3] These studies broadly relate to the variety of approaches in organizational science, with some extra focus on technological and informational aspects of organizations. Based on an inductive analysis, we grouped these papers under eight variables: administrative culture, organizational structure, actions of organizational actors, stakeholder environment, management interventions, technology, policy ideas, and design principles. On the basis of our analysis, we will present a heuristic model for understanding the diverse antecedents of meso-level transparency. A summary of antecedents is found in Figure 4.

### Management Interventions

Management interventions attract a great deal of attention from the literature, likely because they provide a relatively clear and "actionable" path to improve transparency strategies. We found five different types:

---

[3] In many publications, transparency is not separated from other outcomes of information interventions in government organizations. Many authors either discuss transparency and accountability together or they discuss transparency, participation, and collaboration as a set of desirable outcomes. The antecedents then refer to the combined outcomes and not only to transparency.

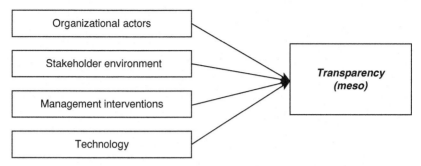

**Figure 4** Antecedents of meso-level transparency[4]

1. Some of these interventions are generic management instruments such as performance management, organizational strategic planning, public planning, knowledge management, and project design (e.g. Ingrams 2018).

2. A second group of interventions is specific management interventions for strengthening transparency such as "precommitment" (Meijer et al. 2014), providing assistance to citizens (Thornton and Thornton 2013), "transparency-by-design" (Janssen et al. 2017), developing training programs for stakeholders (Kimball 2011), and holding open meetings (Piotrowski and Borry 2010).

3. A third group of interventions – online procurement and financial instruments – is specifically related to financial transparency. Al-Aama (2012) highlights that the use of online tools for procurement is a means to increase the transparency of government procurement and Rose and Smith (2012) find that the use of financial instruments – budget stabilization funds – increases the transparency of revenues.

4. A fourth group of interventions focuses on design principles for realizing transparency, addressing both organizational and technological aspects. Dawes (2010), for example, concludes that stewardship and usefulness are fundamental information policy principles for information-based transparency.

5. A final group of interventions focuses on strengthening the capacity and willingness of organizational actors to realize transparency. Cerrillo-i-Martínez (2011) identifies the following managerial practices: reuse licenses, codes of conduct, quality labels and terms and conditions, content rate systems, and early warning and correction mechanisms.

---

[4] In addition, one paper focuses on the relation between actual and perceived transparency and two papers cover a broad variety of factors.

## Technology

Transparency has been strongly linked with the development of technology for a long time (Meijer 2009b). Improvements in technological capacities to store and disseminate information have led to a discussion about its potential to improve government transparency. We found papers focusing on (1) websites and portals and (2) social media:

1. Seven papers investigate the role of websites and portals and generally find that organizational and policy measures are needed to have websites that truly foster transparency (e.g. Caba Pérez et al. 2005; Yavuz and Welch 2014; Lourenço 2015). Other policy elements are strategic alignment with the institutional setting, incentives for adoption, and incremental implementation (Chen 2012).
2. Social media are generally seen as a tool to generate transparency. Bonson et al. (2012), for example, show that the usage of social media tools in EU local governments indeed contributes to government transparency. Gunawong's (2015) study of the Thai public sector, however, shows that only a small fraction of public agencies actively use social media, and therefore, in practice, social media do not contribute to government transparency.

## Actions of Organizational Actors

Five papers investigated the actions of specific organizational actors as an antecedent of transparency. These papers focused on political leadership, managerial/administrative leadership, and the role of government communicators. Szabo et al. (2016) analyze the literature and conclude that political leadership is one of the key antecedents. In addition, managerial action is identified as being important to realizing transparency. Larbi et al. (2019) examine the extent to which the COEs in Ghana comply with the transparency in the Public Procurement Act. They find that the average level of compliance with the transparency provisions is 77.4 percent. They stress that people in managerial positions in all sectors need to try to comply with the transparency provisions in the act to help fight corruption. However, management action is not always geared toward generating more transparency. Roberts (2009) investigates the use of the Right to Information Act in India. He finds that uneven bureaucratic indifference or outright hostility toward the act constrains the usage of this act. Ruijer (2017) investigated the role of government communication officials in the production of government transparency in the United States and the Netherlands. Her research confirms the key role of these professionals and shows that government communication officials can enhance but also occasionally distort transparency. These four papers, however, do not explicitly analyze the interaction between larger institutional structures and actions of organizational actors. This omission is dealt with by Ruijer et al. (2020) in their work on strategic responses to institutional pressure. Ruijer et al. (2020) show how open data practices result from strategic responses to broader institutional pressures for government transparency. This paper illustrates the importance of investigating the interaction between institutional pressures and organizational responses to understand transparency outcomes.

## Stakeholder Environment

The idea behind a focus on the stakeholder environment is that pressure from and collaboration with external stakeholders will force or stimulate the organization to strengthen its transparency efforts. Four papers specifically focus on pressure and expectations from citizens and these papers consistently show that awareness and citizen pressure stimulates transparency. Avery and Graham (2013), for example, study how social media are used by local governments in the United States to enhance government transparency. They collected data from more than 450 local government officials from municipalities across the United States. Based on their study, they identified citizen expectations of government social media usage as one of the key antecedents. Another group of stakeholders is other public organizations. Heimstädt and Dobusch (2018) study the introduction of open data in the Berlin city administration. They show that transparency is constructed through interorganizational negotiation processes in the field. Chen and Chang (2020) study online transparency for open government to identify the conditions affecting the behavior of public agencies. They conclude that the lack of policy conflict is a necessary condition for information provision.

## Other Antecedents

Two papers covered the role of administrative culture as an antecedent of meso-level transparency at different levels: the administrative tradition of a country and the administrative culture of an organization.[5] Ortiz-Rodríguez et al. (2018) studied online transparency regarding the sustainability of public policies in sixty-two local government organizations in the United Kingdom, Ireland, and Southern Europe and found that the prevailing administrative tradition may influence the degree of transparency of local governments. In their meta-analysis of antecedents

---

[5] Meso- and macro-level transparency meet in research into the administrative culture since this concept refers both to a national culture and also to the specific translation of the national culture in an organization. The national culture does not determine the organizational culture but provides an important context for it.

of fiscal transparency, Bolívar et al. (2013) identified the moderator variable, administrative culture, as one of the most influential variables.

Remarkably, only one paper in our sample focused specifically on the structure of an organization. Pina and Torres (2019) investigate to what extent corporate governance structures influence the online transparency of Spanish Central Government Agencies. Their main conclusion is that the presence of independent directors and women on the boards of directors is the most important explanatory factor of online transparency.

The overview shows that certain variables have received much more emphasis in the literature than others: there is a strong emphasis on management interventions and technology as antecedents of transparency. This fits a prescriptive discourse of organizing technology to realize more transparency. Few studies pay specific attention to the interactions between the various antecedents. Exceptions are the study by Ruijer et al. (2019), which analyzes the strategic responses of actors to institutional pressure for transparency, and the study by Avery and Graham (2013) of government officials' perceptions of social media effectiveness. We conclude that the literature provides an extensive overview of the various antecedents, but more research is needed to understand how all the elements interact in specific contextual situations so that we can develop a comprehensive model of the antecedents of government transparency.

## 5.4 What Are the Implications of Meso-Level Transparency?

In total, we identified fourteen studies that examined the implications of meso-level transparency and in addition we found five studies that examined transparency both as a dependent and independent variable. Based on an inductive analysis, we grouped these papers into three categories: implications for the organization, implications for stakeholders, and implications for the relations between organization and stakeholders. A summary is provided in Figure 5.

### Implications for the Internal Organization

Internal implications are effects of transparency on the functioning of government organizations. A core argument of transparency proponents is the purported wholesome effect of "shining a bright light" on how government organizations function. We found studies on the effect of transparency on management decisions, financial decisions, the scale of government, and risk management.

1. Rauh (2016) analyzes the effect of transparency on management decisions about allocating funding and, in contrast with the theoretical expectation that

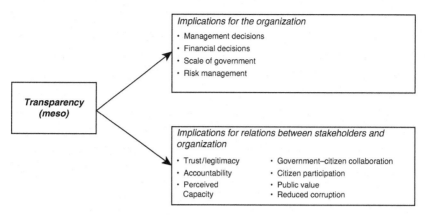

**Figure 5** Overview of main effects of government transparency from meso-level perspective[6]

managers act in an anticipatory manner, they find that managers are more concerned with immediate financial needs.

2. Alt et al. (2002) studied the effect of transparency on the scale of government and conclude that fiscal transparency increases the scale of government since voters entrust greater resources to politicians when fiscal institutions are more transparent.

3. Meijer (2005) analyzes whether transparency results in better risk management and concludes that transparency puts pressure on governments and companies and stimulates them into performing better.

These studies show that transparency is a double-edged sword. On the one hand, greater transparency results in greater awareness and anticipation of the environment of the organization, which may result in a push for better performance. At the same time, there are indications that transparency results in some sort of "myopia": government organizations increase their focus on short-term measures that may immediately increase the popularity of the organization while losing sight of the long-term and broader picture.

### Implications for Stakeholders

External implications are effects of transparency on stakeholders of government organizations. These external implications can be threatening (invasion of privacy) but also supportive (better access to government information).

---

[6] In addition, one paper focuses on the relation between actual and perceived transparency and two papers cover a broad variety of factors.

1. A threat of transparency for stakeholders concerns the infringement of privacy. Graham et al. (2016) find that appropriately handling the tension between transparency and privacy depends on executive leadership, consistent and sound legal advice, and assessment of risk tolerance at the agency level.
2. Cucciniello and Nasi (2014) indicate that the practice of transparency is still linked to the need to comply with legal obligations, not necessarily meeting citizens. They observe a gap between the levels of transparency of governments and the needs of citizens for government information.

## Implications for Relations between Stakeholders and Organization

Relational implications are effects of transparency on the relations between the government organizations and external stakeholders. In the literature, we found different sorts of implications: trust/legitimacy, accountability, perceived capacity, collaboration, citizen participation, and public value. These implications all concern citizens' and stakeholders' perceptions of and connections with government.

1. The first implication concerns trust and legitimacy, to which a large body of the literature has devoted attention (Cucciniello et al. 2017). Generally, studies paint a picture of a strongly context-dependent relation. For instance, Porumbescu (2017) studied the relation between transparency and trust and found a complex pattern depending on the medium used for transparency: a positive relation for social media but no significant relationship for websites. D'onza et al.'s (2017) analysis of the anti-corruption plans of a sample of Italian local governments shows that this type of disclosure might be a way of repairing organizational legitimacy after an occurrence of corruption.
2. The second relational implication is accountability. In many papers, a positive relation between transparency and accountability is assumed rather than investigated and the empirical evidence is less straightforward. Bolívar et al. (2007) show how governmental financial disclosures on the Internet have become a tool for the public to assess financial accountability. Worthy (2015) offers evidence that local government spending data have driven some accountability but the relation between transparency and accountability is complex and unpredictable.
3. The third implication is collaboration between government and citizens. Harrison et al. (2012) regard better collaboration also as an outcome of government transparency and Bertot et al. (2014) highlight that open

government presents a range of opportunities to strengthen collaboration and innovation which can result in real-time solutions to challenges in agriculture, health, or transportation.

4. The fourth implication is improved citizen participation. Again, citizen participation is often used next to transparency rather than as an outcome of it. Still, some publications highlight the effects of transparency on citizen participation but the evidence is mixed. Chun and Cho (2012) conclude that the use of specific online tools did lead to public awareness and understanding, but that it did not result in increased participation. This is in line with older work by Meijer from 2005 who analyzed whether transparency of physical risks results in more citizen engagement. He concludes that few citizens look at the risk maps and, as a consequence, citizen engagement is not strengthened.

5. Fifth, transparency can contribute to a reduction of corruption in the public sector. Although this is a central theme in debates about transparency (e.g. Bauhr and Grimes 2017), there is not a lot of work in this area from the meso-level perspective. Arya and Sharma (2014) highlight how transparency can help to reduce corruption in the Province of Rajasthan in India. Empowered (CSOs helped to use the public information to curb corruption in government.

This overview clearly indicates that the implications of transparency are mixed. The literature highlights how transparency is generally seen as an instrument that strengthens certain outcomes (e.g. information seeking) but also has a negative impact on other outcomes (e.g. privacy). The implications for broader outcomes such as management decisions, accountability, trust, legitimacy, and perceived capacity are far from straightforward. Often only specific forms of transparency seem to "work," or only when accompanied by other organizational policies. Finally, the literature highlights that transparency has an effect on not only the organization or the stakeholders but also on their relations. The whole social system in and around a government organization is influenced by transparency and these social relations are being rearranged and restructured in often unexpected ways.

## 5.5 Main Findings

Two conclusions are taken from this review of empirical research on organizational transparency.

### *Broad Conceptual Mapping but Limited Empirical Evidence*

We found that the term "transparency" is used as an umbrella concept that covers a broad variety of empirical practices among which government websites are dominant. The mapping resulted in a broad range of relations but the evidence for the different relations is limited and mixed. The mapping of the antecedents highlighted a variety of antecedents that we know from the literature on (administrative) organizations: administrative culture, organizational structure, actions of organizational actors, stakeholder environment, management interventions, and technology. In terms of the implications, we found a range of implications that form key aspects of public administration and good governance: trust/legitimacy, accountability, perceived capacity, collaboration between government and citizens, citizen participation, and reduced corruption. In addition, we found some aspects that are directly related to organizational functioning (management decisions, financial decisions, scale of government, and risk management) and some aspects directly related to citizens (privacy and information seeking). Generally, it seems that transparency does reduce corruption although we found only two meso-level-oriented studies investigating this topic. With regard to the other implications, the effects of transparency are subdued and context-dependent at best.

### *Methodological Richness Reflects Complex Phenomenon but Hampers Knowledge Accumulation*

We also have a set of methodological conclusions. Overall the meso-level perspective has a balanced methodological approach and there is not one dominant way of investigating transparency from this perspective. For instance, many of the publications that we analyzed in this section present the results of individual case studies. These studies focus specifically on individual cases such as Toronto (Spicer 2017), Berlin (Heimstädt and Dobusch 2018), Jeddah (Al-Aama 2012), and Seoul (Chun and Cho 2012) to study the antecedents and implications of meso-level transparency. At the same time, we also find a number of quantitative studies that systematically compare government organizations in countries such as Spain (Bolívar et al. 2007; Pina and Torres 2019), the United States (Alt et al. 2002; Avery and Graham 2013), Japan (Ito 2002), and the United Kingdom (Worthy 2015). Although methodological diversity is praiseworthy because it helps us getting a rich understanding of transparency practices and implications, a drawback here is the lack of knowledge accumulation. Finally, an overall finding is that the publications cover practices in many different countries around the world: as opposed to some other research areas, our academic understanding is thus not only based on European and American studies.

## 5.6 Research Directions

### *Empirical Research Needs to Provide More Robust Evidence for the Different Relations*

This section has shown that a variety of antecedents and implications of meso-level transparency have been studied. This diversity of research at the meso-level notwithstanding, there is still a need for more and richer studies into each of the relations that we identified since the evidentiary basis for them is still thin. By extension, the number of publications per specific antecedent or specific implication is still very limited. Even well-known relations, such as the impact of transparency on accountability, have only been investigated in a few empirical studies. The upshot of the lack of attention is that our understanding of transparency from the meso perspective is not robust – we rely heavily on limited evidence. Given the important role organizations play, as the entities charged with implementing transparency, further research from the meso perspective that offers insight into how transparency is operationalized and enhanced, along with when and why transparency initiatives bring about specific implications is essential to efforts to create durable theory.

### *Interactions between Different Variables Need to be Investigated*

A second point for further research concerns the interactions between the different variables and the various feedback loops between transparency, antecedents, and outcomes. How do, for example, citizen engagement and levels of corruption interact in a push for greater transparency, and how does, consequently, higher transparency stimulate more citizen engagement and limit corruption? This inattention to mechanisms that underlie how transparency functions from a meso perspective is problematic because, as was discussed earlier, it limits our understanding of why, for example, transparency is essential for achieving good governance outcomes in some contexts, but not others. These mechanisms, particularly at the meso level, are difficult to capture, yet truly important to understand if we are to move beyond a context-dependent understanding of transparency.

### *Causal Mechanisms Need to be Tested Empirically*

A third point relates to better understanding the causal structure of transparency antecedents and implications. At present, much of the research from this perspective is exploratory and employs a variety of transparency measures. This diversity at the meso level raises issues related to measurement equivalence and provokes questions of whether observed effects actually relate to transparency or a related construct. Related, meso-level research also points to endogeneity in the relationship between determinants and implications. For example, some papers see citizen engagement as the outcome of transparency, whereas others see transparency as the outcome of citizen engagement. While it is certainly possible for something to be both an antecedent and implication of transparency, thinking more critically about the causal structure of relationships related to transparency will offer a more systematic understanding of transparency from the meso perspective.

## 6 The Micro-Level Perspective on Transparency

### 6.1 Introducing the Micro-Level Perspective on Transparency

Micro-level research refers to research that focuses on interactions between individuals, such as individual cognitions, attributes, intentions, behaviors, feelings, and beliefs (Jilke et al. 2019). In doing so, micro-level-oriented research is often informed by theories about psychological processes (Grimmelikhuijsen et al. 2017). The classic work of Herbert Simon on administrative behavior forms the basis for this approach (Simon 1947a). According to Simon (1947b) "[f]or the man who wishes to explore the pure science of administration, it will dictate at least a thorough grounding in social psychology" (1947: 202). His work on bounded rationality – that is, due to cognitive and practical constraints administrators will search for satisfactory instead of ideal policy solutions – was groundbreaking and has had a continued influence on this line of research.

In micro-level research, the unit of analysis focuses "on psychological processes within or between individuals" and is embedded within the meso (e.g. organizational) and macro (e.g. institutional roles) levels (Kozlowski and Klein 2000). From this point of view, the micro-level perspective on transparency studies the effects and determinants of government transparency from the point of view of individuals, which can be individual citizens but also other individual stakeholders such as government officials, journalists, or activists.

An example of how transparency is studied at the micro-level is by De Fine Licht (2011). She designed an experiment where one group was given no information at all on a certain decision-making procedure in public health care (reflecting a nontransparent decision-making process) and six groups were exposed with different descriptions of a decision-making procedure. She found that the groups exposed to decision-making information tended to have less trust in the Swedish health care system than the nontransparent control group. This is an example of the micro level as the unit of analysis centers on individuals and how their attitudes are affected by decision-making transparency.

Although studies such as these have provided fresh insights into the debate on the effects of transparency, the micro-level perspective on government transparency is relatively scarce when compared to the two other perspectives. Our literature review encompassing almost three decades of studies on transparency shows that during this period forty-three articles (out of 244 in total) on government transparency took a micro-level perspective (see Table 4 for an overview). In this section, we provide an overview of how transparency is measured (Section 6.2), what kind of antecedents (Section 6.3), and implications (Section 6.4) of transparency are identified at the micro level. In Section 6.5, we summarize the main findings from this level and we finalize the section by formulating some research directions (Section 6.6).

## 6.2 How Is Transparency Measured at the Micro Level?

Of the forty-three articles in which transparency was investigated at the micro level, sixteen used perceptual measures. The other twenty-seven articles used a variety of objective measures. Most of these measures are found in experimental or game-theoretical studies.

The *perceptual measures of transparency* are mostly unidimensional. Cicatiello et al. (2018) use general perceptions from an existing index of the World Economic Forum asking private sector top managers whether government information is easily accessible. Some studies directly ask whether people perceive government to be transparent (e.g. Estrada and Bastida 2020), while others specifically ask for certain core aspects of transparency, such as the perceived proactive release of government information (Wu et al. 2017). Sometimes, specific information is assessed, for instance, Zuo and Wheeler (2019) asked industrial company managers about their perceptions of air pollution emission data.

Only six articles in the perceptual category explicitly operationalize transparency as a multidimensional construct. Piotrowski and Van Ryzin (2007) were one of the first to develop a multidimensional scale of perceived transparency. They found that people had different perceptions of transparency on national safety, fiscal transparency, and what they call "principled openness." More recently, authors have also used multidimensional constructs, but with slightly different dimensions. Park and Blenkinsopp (2017) developed a multidimensional scale with different dimensions for citizens and administrators. Jordan et al. (2017) measured transparency by letting laymen rank and rate popular financial reports and found dimensions such as comprehension, access, and appearance are part of financial transparency. Cucciniello et al. (2015) focus on a scale gauging perceptions of institutional, political, financial, and service transparency. De Boer and Eshuis (2018) and De Boer et al. (2018) build on Grimmelikhuijsen and Meijer's (2014) work by explicitly measuring

**Table 4** Summary of literature review micro-level perspective on transparency

| | |
|---|---|
| Summary | Forty-three articles were published between 1990 and 2019 (out of 244) |
| Definition of micro-level perspective | The micro-level perspective on transparency studies the implications and antecedents of government transparency from the point of view of individuals, which can be individual citizens but also other individual stakeholders such as journalists or activists |
| How transparency is studied | Independent variable (6) <br> Dependent variable (37) |
| How is transparency measured | • Perceptual measures (16) <br> ◦ Unidimensional perception (10) <br> ◦ Multidimensional perception (6) <br> • Objective measures (27) <br> ◦ Manipulated/fabricated website or news content (14) <br> ◦ Semi-objective survey data (2) <br> ◦ Objective measure (1) <br> ◦ Objective and perceptual combined (1) <br> ◦ Reported exposure to government information (1) <br> ◦ Real performance data (1) <br> ◦ Text messages (1) <br> ◦ FOI requests (1) <br> ◦ Television show (1) |
| Main substantive themes (only included when there are more than three studies) | Implications <br> • Trust/legitimacy (17) <br> • (Perceived) performance (10) <br> • Government integrity (3) <br> Antecedents <br> • Gap between actual and desired transparency features |

transparency as a multifaceted construct with perceptions of regulators of (1) completeness, (2) coloring, and (3) usability. Finally, Cucciniello and Nasi (2014) combine perceived transparency with actual transparency of local government websites.

The second branch of measures, *objective measures of transparency*, is much more diverse, which probably relates to the very different methodologies that are used to probe the effects of transparency. Of the twenty-five articles using objective measures, five use cross-sectional (nonexperimental) data. For instance, Grimmelikhuijsen and Meijer (2015) use reported exposure to Twitter messages of the police, and Porumbescu (2015) has a similar approach but for exposure to government websites. Mason et al. (2014) have used actual performance data from the police to measure transparency. Finally, there are two studies in the area of budget transparency. Benito and Bastida (2009) used the OECD International Budget Practices and Procedures Database, which contains objective survey questions about what type of budget information is disclosed. Craveiro and Albano (2017) use the Open Budget Survey of the International Budget Partnership. This survey consists of questions similar to that of the OECD database. Finally, Hyun et al. (2018) use an objective measure of transparency by investigating the extent to which frontline workers report information to citizens in Bangalore.

The other twenty articles in this category are experimental. Three game-theoretical experiments use some kind of information as a way to induce transparency. Azfar and Nelson (2007) use a corruption disclosure and Li et al. (2019) use disclosure of air pollutant emissions. Fox (2007) focuses on the anticipated disclosure of a policy decision. Eleven experiments can be classified as survey experiments. Here a transparency manipulation is embedded in a survey, in the form of a newspaper article (De Fine Licht 2014; De Fine Licht et al. 2014) or as mock government website (e.g. Porumbescu et al. 2017; Piotrowski et al. 2019). In these studies there are different variations in the type of transparency. For instance, Grimmelikhuijsen (2010), De Fine Licht (2014), and Porumbescu and Grimmelikhuijsen (2018) focus on decision-making transparency. In contrast, Grimmelikhuijsen and Meijer (2014) and Grimmelikhuijsen et al. (2013) and Piotrowski et al. (2019) focus on transparency of policy outcomes. Another type of information receiving attention in survey experiments is information about specific policies and policy measures (Porumbescu et al. 2017, 2018).

Finally, there are three field experiments that use real-world occurrences of transparency. Transparency measures here are very diverse. Buntaine et al. (2018) employ text messages about national park management and revenue, Peisakhin (2011) uses FOI requests to see if these help residents of slum dwellers to get food ration cards in time. Finally, Grimmelikhuijsen and Klijn (2015) instructed people to watch a television show about the Dutch judiciary.

Overall, when we look at the way transparency is measured at the micro level, three conclusions come into focus. First, there is a large variety of measures available, both for objective and perceptual operationalizations of transparency. Measures hardly overlap and do not build on each other. From the point of view of knowledge accumulation, this might not seem desirable, at the same time the contextual nature of transparency forces researchers to use specific measures that fit their particular research context. Secondly, these variations occur in various dimensions. There is variation in the type of information that is measured (budget, decision-making, performance), the type of medium (websites, television, newspapers, FOI requests), and the properties of the information itself (completeness, usability). Thirdly, there is a remarkable difference in transparency as measured as an independent or as a dependent variable. Especially with regard to perceptual measures we see that transparency as a dependent variable is treated as a multidimensional, rich, concept, whereas as an independent variable it is much more often treated as a unidimensional construct. Overall, the micro-oriented literature is diverse and rich in transparency measures, which may limit knowledge accumulation but at the same time allows for meaningful interpretations of transparency in its specific context. In the next section, we will outline substantive findings regarding transparency as a dependent variable (Section 6.3) and independent variable (Section 6.4).

## 6.3 Transparency as a Dependent Variable from a Micro-Level Perspective

We identified six empirical articles on the determinants of transparency. This suggests that the micro-level determinants receive little attention in the literature. Figure 6 provides an overview of the determinants of government transparency.

When we examine these articles we see that they are split between citizen-centric and government-centric approaches:

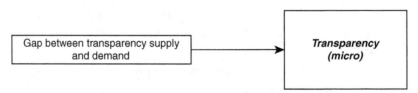

**Figure 6** Main determinants of (perceived) transparency from the micro-level perspective

1. The limited number of studies from a *citizen-centric approach* investigates citizen perceptions of transparency and consistently identifies gaps between transparency needs and actual transparency as offered on government websites. For instance, works by Cucciniello, Nasi and colleagues (2014, 2015) assess citizen needs for transparency to improve effective transparency amongst Italian municipalities. Interestingly, they find that citizens rate transparency of service delivery and local finances as most important, yet municipal websites tend to publish other types of information. A similar approach was taken by Jordan et al. (2017) who identified information qualities to improve fiscal transparency and then does content analyses on government websites. The article concludes that websites are strong on information availability of data but weak on comprehensibility of information. Finally, Piotrowski and Van Ryzin (2007) not only investigate transparency perceptions on various dimensions of transparency, but also the individual-level determinants that correlate with these dimensions. In general, they find that political engagement and liberal ideology increase transparency demands while, in contrast, confidence in government leaders decreases this demand.

2. Three articles were found to have a *government-centric approach*. Like the citizen-centric approach, these studies show that the implementation of transparency at the individual level is complicated and that there is a significant gap between what information citizens want and what information they "get" from government. Meijer (2005) looked at individual and organizational barriers to online risk transparency. He finds that transparency does not directly lead to a better-informed citizenry as people are generally not interested in this information. Another example is a study by Hyun et al. (2018), which shows that government workers have limited time and attention to implement this transparency policy.

It is worth noting that we found one study taking an explicit combination of the citizen-centric and government-centric approaches. Park and Blenkinsopp (2017) fielded a survey amongst citizens and public employees to compare their views of transparency. The authors find that both groups have different understandings of transparency. Public employees perceived transparency as consisting of reliable and accessible information, whereas citizens view transparency as accessibility but also in terms of usefulness. This suggests that public employees adopt a somewhat narrower view of transparency: it should be reliable and accessible, whereas for citizens it should primarily be useful.

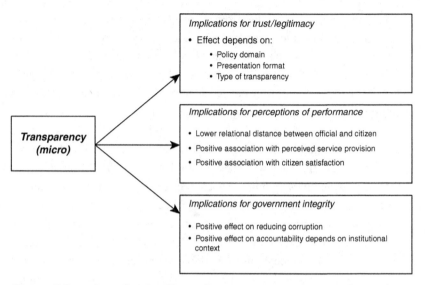

**Figure 7** Overview of main effects of government transparency from micro-level perspective

## 6.4 Transparency as an Independent Variable from a Micro-Level Perspective

Much more attention in the literature is paid to the effects of transparency (thirty-seven articles). This branch of the literature is dominated by the citizen perspective so we will not discuss a government-centric approach separately the way we did in Section 6.3. To make the description of the literature more insightful we identified four main substantive clusters that were found in the literature. Figure 7 provides an overview of the effects of transparency identified at the micro level.

### Effects on Trust and (Perceived) Legitimacy

One of the main debates on transparency is its relationship with trust in government (Erkkilä 2020). Transparency policies are often developed explicitly to strengthen citizen trust in government (Hood and Heald 2006; Cucciniello et al. 2017). It may come as no surprise that the largest cluster of studies is on trust, legitimacy, and related attitudes toward government (seventeen studies). These studies are citizen-centric and, overall, they paint a mixed picture of the possible effects of transparency on trust and legitimacy.

Within this cluster we see a relatively strong presence of experimental studies. Typically, these are survey experiments that manipulate information content or presentation compared to a control group and then gauge attitudinal measures on trust, legitimacy, or acceptance. There is not a single clear conclusion emerging from these experiments, yet they do show that the effect of transparency on trust is highly context-dependent. For instance, several studies now indicate that the policy domain in which transparency is placed matters (e.g. Porumbescu et al. 2017). For instance, De Fine Licht (2014) finds that the policy domain and type of transparency matter for the effect of transparency. Transparency about "taboo" decision trade-offs such as health-care quality versus expenditure tends to have a negative effect on decision acceptance. In contrast, "routine" trade-offs such as park quality versus expenditure may not yield such a negative effect.

Next to the policy domain, Porumbescu and colleagues have found that the specific presentation format affects decision acceptance and policy understanding. In a survey experiment, Porumbescu et al. (2017) found that simple bulleted information tends to be better understood than when the same information was presented in a running text. Interestingly, this increased understanding did not lead to more, but less, policy support.

Finally, institutional contexts seem to moderate transparency effects, too. Grimmelikhuijsen et al. (2013) showed that transparency has a more pronounced negative effect in South Korea yet not in the Netherlands. Also, certain institutions seem to be better off than others. It seems that when less politicized institutions are better able to increase citizen trust when they exhibit some kind of transparency. Grimmelikhuijsen and Klijn (2015) found in a field experiment that court transparency had a positive effect on trust in judges. Furthermore, Grimmelikhuijsen et al. (2019) find a similar positive result for regulatory agencies in the health care and education domain. This is in contrast to the subdued or even negative findings in experiments on more central government organizations, such as local or federal governments.

Next to the experimental cluster, there have been several publications using observational data in this area. In contrast to the mixed findings produced by the aforementioned experiments, these studies tend to find overall positive relations between (perceived) transparency and trust in government (e.g. Porumbescu 2015). For instance, Kim and Lee (2012) used survey data collected in Seoul and found positive associations between e-participation, transparency, and trust in local government. Similarly, Wu et al. (2017) find that government transparency is positively related to perceived social equity and that trust in government. Other studies echo these positive associations about e-government use (Welch et al. 2005), police legitimacy (Grimmelikhuijsen and Meijer 2015), and political efficacy (Cicatiello et al. 2018).

What can we conclude from this cluster of studies? First, there is no straightforward positive or negative relation between transparency and trust. Nonexperimental studies provide evidence that transparency has the potential to increase positive views of government, yet these studies generally have the potential for omitted variables or common source bias (e.g. Favero and Bullock 2015). In contrast, experimental studies show that the effect of transparency depends on various contextual variables: policy domain, institutional character-istics, and even presentation format affect trust in government. At the same time, these are mostly survey experiments that have the disadvantages of being more artificial and modest in terms of treatment which could limit their external validity (Gaines et al. 2007). Field experiments may be "the best of both worlds" yet given that these are generally time-consuming and expensive to carry out, we only found a handful in our search.

### Effects on (Perceived) Performance

In total ten studies in this cluster were found. Overall, these articles indicate a limited yet positive relation between transparency and (perceived) performance. Of these ten studies, three had a government-centric approach. We first discuss the government-centric articles.

The three government-centric articles focus on the effects of transparency on street-level bureaucrats. De Boer and colleagues show in two articles that increased transparency in regulatory agencies increases the relational distance between regulators and regulatees, but inspectors in these agencies still perceive a higher perceived performance (De Boer and Eshuis 2018). In a similar study, De Boer et al. (2018) find that perceived disclosure decreases the resistance that food safety inspectors experience during inspections. Fox (2007) carried out a controlled lab experiment to gauge the effect of increased transparency on policy choices. Fox concludes that transparency induces perverse reputational concerns among policymakers. When policymakers expect their choices to be widely published they tend to select policies that what they believe make them perceived as unbiased and not necessarily what is best for their constituents.

The other seven articles take a citizen-centric approach and mostly deal with some form of citizen satisfaction with government performance. In this cluster mostly positive associations with transparency are found. For example, Hong (2014) finds that increased perceptions of transparency correlate with better perceived citizen–government relations. Likewise, Porumbescu (2017) finds a positive relation between transparency and satisfaction with public service provision. At the same time, experimental evidence from Uganda finds no effect on sending information text message on various perceptions, such as citizen satisfaction (Buntaine et al. 2018)

Overall, evidence from micro-level studies points to a positive relation between transparency and performance-related measures, both from the perspective of government officials and citizens. Perhaps citizen trust is less amenable to positive change. Another explanation is that, in contrast with the trust cluster, there were hardly any experimental studies and there might be some issues with endogeneity with studies on government performance. This is also highlighted by the fact that the only experimental study in this cluster did not find a clear positive effect on performance (Fox 2007).

### Effects on Corruption and Accountability

It is commonly assumed that government transparency positively relates to accountability and to (reduced) corruption (e.g. Hood and Heald 2006). Interestingly, not many studies on the micro-level focus on these two themes. We found four empirical studies on the effects of transparency on corruption and accountability. Although this cluster of studies is very small, we discuss this part of the literature given the importance of both themes in the debate at the macro and meso levels.

The three studies with a micro-level focus have overall found positive effects on reduced corruption. Park and Blenkinsopp (2011) find that higher levels of perceived transparency are associated with less perceived corruption. In addition, two experiments corroborate this positive association. A field experiment in India finds that transparency legislation helps slum dwellers to get food stamps in time without having to resort to bribery (Peisakhin 2011). Likewise, Azfar and Nelson (2007) showed that corruption is reduced with higher levels of disclosure.

Bauhr and Grimes (2014) combine a micro level with a macro-level perspective. Transparency was predicted to deter corruption in part by expanding the possibilities for societal accountability. They find that transparency only leads to calling out corruption when corruption in a country is not endemic. In other words, if corruption in a country is widespread more transparency will only lead to more cynicism and a resigned public while in countries with incidental corruption more transparency leads to higher levels of societal accountability.

Overall, this indicates that transparency has the potential to reduce corrupt practices and lead to more accountability, yet the country context should be taken into account as a moderating variable.

## 6.5 Main Findings

Most of the micro-oriented literature tends to focus on the effects of transparency on individual citizens, while there is limited attention for effects on government officials or for the factors and dynamics that shape transparency at the micro level. This predominant focus also drives the main conclusions of this section. We can draw three main substantive conclusions from this literature overview

### 1. There is often a Mismatch between What Information Governments Offer and What Citizens Want

One key finding is the discrepancy between the informational needs of citizens and information supply. Studies have shown that citizens want concrete and usable information on things that are directly important to them such as service delivery (e.g. Cucciniello and Nasi 2014) yet government officials are more concerned with providing detailed, accurate (yet less usable) information (e.g. Park and Blenkinsopp 2017). One of the consequences of this gap is that citizens hardly use government information (Meijer 2005).

### 2. Transparency Generally Has Positive Effects on Reducing Corruption and Improving Government Performance

Nearly all studies we found reported a positive effect of transparency on reducing corruption and government performance as experienced by individual citizens. This is interesting as these have been one two of the major goals often promulgated with the introduction of new government transparency policies. Similar positive associations between transparency and perceived performance are reported by studies on citizens (e.g. Porumbescu 2015, 2017) and government officials (e.g. De Boer and Eshuis 2018). One caveat concerning this conclusion is that the "performance cluster" is mostly based on cross-sectional research and that it is not possible to make causal claims based on this type of research. This is different for the "corruption cluster." We find only a handful of empirical studies but there is a mix of survey and experimental evidence. From a micro perspective, individuals experience less corruption when there is more government transparency, such as through more extensive help with filing FOI requests to receive food stamps (Peisakhin 2011).

### 3. There Is Mixed Evidence on the Relation between Transparency and Trust in Government

A large portion of studies within the micro-level literature has focused on the relation between transparency and trust, yet the outcomes are not straightforward. On the one hand there are studies that consistently find positive associations between (perceptions of) government transparency and trust (e.g. Kim and Lee 2012), yet other – mostly experimental – studies provide evidence showing that the relation is much more ambiguous (Cucciniello et al. 2017). This indicates that this discrepancy may at least partly be due to a methodological artefact. Indeed, cross-sectional studies linking transparency perceptions with other attitudinal measures, such as trust, are more likely to reveal positive associations. This is a well-known issue brought forward in methodological literature (e.g. Favero and Bullock 2015) and the direct comparison with experimental results provides some evidence that this positive skew is also present in transparency research. Overall, the effect of transparency on trust, is highly context-dependent and to think carefully about contextual concerns and what informational demands are important to citizens under particular circumstances.

## 6.6 Research Directions

### *Research Micro-Level Determinants and Dynamics That Shape Transparency or Perceptions of Transparency*

The micro-level literature predominantly focuses on transparency as an independent variable. In other words, there is ample research into the effect of transparency on other variables such as trust, performance, or satisfaction. In contrast, what determines individual perception of transparency has received limited attention so far. For instance, next to identifying information-seeking needs of citizens (e.g. Park and Blenkinsopp 2017) it would be interesting to have more systematic research to get a better understanding of the determinants and dynamics that affect these individual perceptions. Such understanding would be beneficial since it gives a better sense of what kind of information is needed by what type of citizen.

### *Research Individual Level Dynamics of Government Officials*

Another predominant focus in the literature is the citizen-centric approach, whereas a government-centric approach received limited attention. Currently, less than a handful of studies provide insights into how government officials perceive transparency measures or, even more importantly, how individual civil servants shape and construct transparency in their work. One study (Hyun et al. 2018) suggests that barriers to implementing transparency policies can hinge on very personal issues of government officials, such as their family situation and the time they have to work on implementing a transparency fix. We need more micro-level studies like this to get a fuller picture of individual barriers restraining government officials in order to be informed about what can be done to overcome them.

## *Employ Field Experiments and Mixed Methods to Combine Internal with External Validity*

The third research direction relates to the discrepancy in findings between cross-sectional and experimental studies. Earlier on in this section, we noted cross-sectional studies are not suitable for causal claims and might exaggerate potential positive associations between transparency and citizen trust. At the same time, survey experimental studies show a much more nuanced and mixed picture yet these types of designs are more artificial and the external validity of survey experiments such as these have been debated in the literature (Gaines et al. 2007). To combine the strength of both approaches, future research may go in the direction of explicit mixed methods design in which the same transparency initiative is studied by both experiments and other methods. In addition, we found only a few field experiments concerning transparency (e.g. Buntaine et al. 2018; Peisakhin 2011), and this type of experimental design can be helpful in improving the external validity of some of the causal claims made surrounding government transparency (John 2020).

## 7 Linking and Integrating Research on Government Transparency

### 7.1. Why Do We Need a Layered Approach to Government Transparency?

Despite the wealth of research on transparency from micro, meso, and macro perspectives, there have been few attempts to connect these distinct yet related perspectives. This fragmented approach to the study of government transparency not only inhibits theoretical development, but also obscures the contributions of transparency to governing processes. A consequence of this epistemic fragmentation is that transparency "has been identified as the cause of, and solution to, a remarkable range of problems" (Pozen 2020: 326).

The goal of this section is to present a flexible methodology that acknowledges the interrelatedness of the macro, meso, and micro perspectives on government transparency. Core to our argument is a set of relationships between the macro, meso, and micro perspectives on transparency, which are nested within a particular context. As we will explain, the relationships between perspectives are interdependent and variable – changes to one perspective will trigger shifts in the other two. Acknowledging the interrelatedness of these perspectives provides a broader and more structured understanding of transparency by connecting specific practices to the overarching transparency environment.

At a fundamental level, we need to state explicitly that we do not assume neat connections between the macro, meso, and micro perspectives. Emerging patterns at the meso and macro levels may differ from micro patterns through generative mechanisms such as collective action, cultural bias, routines, and so on. We have seen this, for example, in the seemingly contradictory outcomes for the relation between transparency and trust. As we know from systems theory (Skyttner 2005), emerging properties at a higher system level may differ from the properties of the components. This means that specific tensions between findings need to be analyzed both on the basis of theoretical and methodological considerations. Tensions between perspectives can form a key basis for advancing our theoretical understanding of government transparency.

The layered approach to studying transparency we advocate for advances transparency scholarship in two ways. First, as transparency takes root in a growing number of contexts around the world, the explanatory power of existing transparency models struggles to keep pace with the diversity. The layered approach advances efforts to conceptualize and analyze transparency by outlining a contingent, context-driven approach that links the value orientation toward transparency in a particular context to managerial practices and behavioral responses. Second, a layered approach allows scholars to better capture the multifaceted nature of transparency. That is, for evaluations of transparency to meaningfully translate across contexts and perspectives, we need a model capable of connecting regime values to managerial practices to individual behaviors and attitudes.

We explain this layered approach to studying transparency in this final section of the Element. We begin Section 7.2 by discussing how the three levels are complementary and in Section 7.3 we show that by focusing on substantive themes, such as corruption, we can connect and integrate transparency studies from each perspective. Section 7.4 concludes this Element by reflecting on our findings and looking forward to the continued role of government transparency in our societies.

## 7.2 How Micro-, Meso-, and Macro-Level Studies Complement Each Other

### Pattern 1: Micro-Level Research Fills a Crucial Gap by Studying the Implications of Transparency

The discussion of research into transparency at the micro, meso, and macro levels shows an interesting difference in the focus on transparency as an independent or a dependent variable. Research at the micro level mostly focuses on transparency as an independent variable. This variable is, for example, manipulated to investigate how it influences outcomes such as trust, (perceived) performance, and (perceived) corruption. In contrast, most of the research at the meso and macro levels focuses on transparency as a dependent variable. At the meso level, a variety of antecedents – culture, structure, actions of organizational actors, stakeholder environments, management interventions, technology, and societal context – are investigated to explain differences in the level of transparency of countries. At the macro level, the influence of determinants such as technology, pressure, political values, and context is investigated to develop explanations for differences in level of transparency between countries, regions, or cities.

This observation highlights the position of micro-level research – the youngest tradition of the three – in research into transparency. The key contribution of research at the micro level is that it strengthens our academic understanding of the implications of transparency. In older research, the idea that transparency is desirable was a given and there was only a need to investigate the extent to which transparency was actually being realized through legislative frameworks, policies, and organizational actions. There was some attention to implications at the meso and macro levels but this research is relatively scarce. Zooming in on the micro level allows us to test theoretical assumptions in controlled conditions, which is an opportunity we do not have at meso and macro levels.

A challenge for future research is how the insights about the implications of transparency at the micro level can be translated to insights at the meso and macro levels. One can imagine that the outcomes from the research at the micro level can be translated into hypotheses that can be tested and further developed at the meso and macro levels. In view of the fact that new properties may arise at higher levels, it will also be relevant to study and analyze not only implications that are in line with micro-level insights but also seemingly conflicting outcomes

### Pattern 2: Meso and Macro Levels Provide Crucial Insights into the Contextual Nature of Transparency

The discussion of the three levels indicates that there is a more reductionist perspective at the micro level and a more holistic perspective at the meso and macro levels. Research at the micro level aims to generate generalizable insights into the relation between transparency and outcomes such as perceived performance, perceived corruption, and trust in government. This is especially true for the latter, which has been a core focus in a significant number of publications. The evidence, however, points to an inconsistent pattern of findings across different studies, implying outcomes are not always clear. Research at the meso and macro levels helps to interpret the inconsistent pattern of effects identified by research from the micro perspective by putting much more emphasis on the societal, stakeholder, political, and cultural context and emphasizing that these contexts influence the relation between transparency and the various outcomes.

The value of the research at the meso and macro levels is that they help to develop a contextual understanding of both the antecedents and the implications of government transparency. The challenge in linking these perspectives to research on the micro level is that they rely on very different epistemological positions. This does not mean, however, that we should not endeavor to produce insights that identify both generalizable and context-specific patterns. To this end, reductionism in transparency research can be addressed by incorporating a better understanding of contextual conditions to ensure that the outcomes of this type of research are also societally valid, and holistic research can incorporate some key findings from reductionist research to check whether these are also encountered in rich, qualitative research.

Here, we echo the recommendation made by Jilke et al. (2019) on the use of analytical levels in public administration research. First, scholars should be explicit in what their level of analysis is and, second, they should explicitly discuss how levels interact with regard to their topic. This means that a macro-level study on transparency should be explicit in the type of analysis it is presenting and at the same time should discuss how the findings speak to meso- (e.g. policies) and micro-level (e.g. citizen views) questions.

### Pattern 3: Macro and Meso Research Provide Insights into Nominal Transparency and Micro-Level Research into Effective Transparency

The discussion of the three bodies of literature also highlights an interesting difference in the actor's focus. The research at the meso and macro levels mostly focuses on government. The research aims to explain legislative processes, policy development, and organizational actions. The social environment and, more specifically, the role of citizens are seen as relevant but there is little research into perceptions and actions of citizens. In contrast, research at the micro level focuses mostly on citizen perceptions. Experimental research is used to study how transparency influences the perceptions of citizens and, at this level, there is relatively little attention to the perceptions of government officials and street-level bureaucrats.

In other words, the meso- and macro-level bodies of research focus on what Heald calls "nominal transparency" (Heald 2006; Heald 2012). Nominal transparency refers to the formal requirements of transparency and availability of information. The meso and macro levels tend to take state actors as their focal point of study and consequently provide a variety of academic insights into what kind of information governments make available. However, this information might not reach citizens and other stakeholders at all: information might not be read, understood, and processed. This is where micro-level research can provide important insights: it will help to show what kind of transparency is actually effective (Heald 2006).

This observation confirms the need to understand transparency both as a process of information provision and information usage. Research at the macro and meso levels provides an in-depth understanding of the (strategic, partial, mandated) processes of information provision in different contexts. Research at the micro level presents a critical view of this perspective on citizens and emphasizes that we need to build an empirical understanding of these perceptions, rather than simply assuming citizens will seek information to strengthen their democratic position. Connecting the study of both nominal and effective transparency is a key challenge for future research into government transparency.

## 7.3 Connecting Perspectives on Substantive Themes: A Research Agenda

### *A Layered Approach to Studying Transparency for Future Research*

We started this Element with the observation that there is a need for more comprehensive models of transparency to clearly map what we know and do not know about the antecedents and implications of transparency. A variety of insights have been presented in the previous sections and we observed that many themes (e.g. trust, accountability, corruption) were analyzed at different levels and resulted in different insights. Now we will connect these insights through a lens of related substantive themes. Figures 8 and 9 indicate how a layered approach can be used to map and connect micro-, meso-, and macro-level insights. In Figure 8, we highlight the most studied implications of government transparency: accountability, corruption/integrity, trust/legitimacy, performance, and (risk) management. We will discuss each theme and highlight promising avenues for future research.

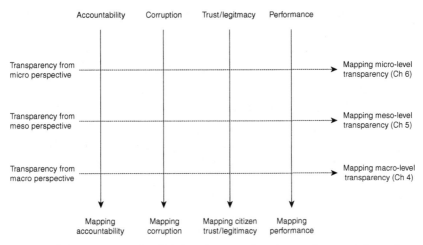

**Figure 8** Transparency implications: connecting perspectives on substantive themes

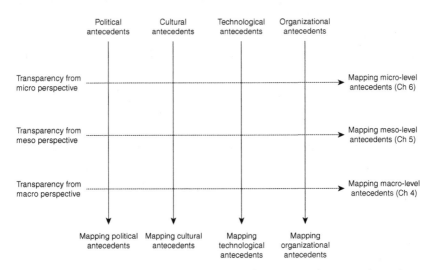

**Figure 9** Transparency antecedents: connecting perspectives on substantive themes

Most transparency research agendas today focus on the intersections of dotted horizontal lines in Figure 8. Within a single perspective, there is an emphasis on one or sometimes two substantive themes. The mapping exercise we carried out sheds light on what is known so far regarding each substantive theme situated on X-axis of the figure. In-depth discussions can be found in each respective section. Throughout this Element we have argued the importance of paying more attention to the vertical lines. By relating government transparency research on substantive themes we can better understand the layered impact each perspective on transparency has on outcomes of interest, such as accountability. The same is true for understanding factors that increase transparency. The themes in Figure 8 are by no means exhaustive, but we do find that throughout the literature these are commonly studied topics in relation to government transparency. Our framework is open in the sense that additional themes can easily be captured in the same logic of the horizontal and vertical lines.

Accountability. From the macro and meso perspective transparency is viewed as integral to efforts to strengthen accountability (Hood 2010). In particular, information disclosure is a core element of political account-ability (Bovens 2007). On the meso level, a positive relationship between transparency and accountability is often assumed, rather than investigated. Worthy (2015) emphasizes the complexities of the relationship between transparency and democratic accountability. His study of the impact of the UK coalition government's transparency agenda indicates that the local government spending data have driven some accountability, but that the relation between transparency and accountability is complex and unpredictable.

The key to understanding this unpredictable relationship may be found in connecting the macro- and meso-level insights to findings at the micro level. Various psychological studies have shown that people will try to avoid embarrassment in public and thus will behave in a way that is in line with what the public expects from them (cf. Lerner and Tetlock 1999). For this to occur, a public official must anticipate that they will be held accountable for their behavior (Overman and Schillemans 2022). Academic research suggests that transparency may not necessarily lead to increased felt account-ability. For instance, many citizens do not care too much about the existence of transparency laws (e.g. Grimmelikhuijsen et al. 2020). Hence, future research may focus on micro-level dynamics between transparency and accountability. At present there is only limited evidence on this relationship, but there is micro-oriented research in both transparency and accountability separately (Porumbescu et al. 2021). As a next step, research programs need to assess how such insights drawn on the micro level can translate "upwards" into meso-level organizational policies and macro-level institutional arrangement.

Corruption/Integrity. Transparency is commonly associated with the integrity and lack of corruption of government officials. Often transparency reforms are called for to reduce corruption. There is some research on the link between transparency and integrity from each perspective that generally points in the same direction. At the macro level, research has shown that increased levels of transparency can reduce corruption, but only if corruption is not endemic and if there are ways for citizens to address corruption. Otherwise, transparency will only lead to cynicism (Bauhr and Grimes 2014). In line with this, one meso-level study shows that transparency can empower CSOs that use public information to curb corruption in India (Peisakhin 2011). At the micro level three studies, with varying methodological approaches, have overall found positive effects on reduced corruption.

Overall, when we connect perspectives for the substantive theme of integrity/corruption we see fairly consistent evidence on the reduction of corruption by means of transparency laws and policies. Future research may focus on solidifying the evidence, especially at the meso and micro level, as there were only a few studies that focus on this relationship from those perspectives.

Legitimacy/trust. In general, micro-level research devotes the most attention to this outcome. There is some macro-level research yet very little at the meso level. What is interesting is that there are mixed findings across the three levels. For instance, experimental studies find that transparency has a negative effect on perceived legitimacy when the information content concerns a "taboo" trade-off (De Fine Licht 2014). On the other hand, when transparency reveals positive procedural cues public trust increases. Also, the body of research on this theme indicates that transparency of less politicized organizations (such as judges or regulatory agencies) tends to generate more trust than more politicized bodies (such as local parliaments or councils; e.g. Grimmelikhuijsen et al. 2019).

Furthermore, some types of transparency may be more effective in engendering legitimacy and trust than others. For instance, explaining the rationale behind decisions retrospectively is more effective than "immediate" transparency in decision-making processes. Such nuances and complexities are in line with macro-level analyses that emphasize the complexity of the relation between transparency and trust/legitimacy. For instance, studies at the macro level have argued that, to understand the relation between transparency and legitimacy, we need to shift our attention away from amounts of information and toward types of information (Roelofs 2019) and even that institutional transparency reforms do not necessarily lead to more public trust (Arellano-Gault 2016).

Performance. In general, studies across the micro, meso, and macro levels are consistent in terms of the associations between government transparency and government performance. At the macro level, studies report that transparency is positively associated with economic indicators, such as the efficiency of economic transparency or the cost of sovereign debt. At the meso level, there is a broad range of performance-related measures, but all are positively related to transparency, such as collaboration, public value, participation, and government capacity. At the micro level, performance tends to be measured using perceptual measures. Despite this difference in measurement, we see that transparency and performance are generally positively related.

To better understand the nature of this relationship, causal evidence on the effect of government transparency on objective performance measures is needed. While objective performance indicators are used at the meso and macro levels, we generally lack causal evidence. Addressing this gap in the literature requires either large-scale field experiments with government organizations (for causal evidence at these levels) and/or complementary causal evidence from micro-level studies using objective indicators. Layering our causal in this way will provide more credible evidence on claims that government transparency indeed causes better performance.

Now that we have discussed how we can obtain novel insights on the implications of transparency by connecting the three perspectives, we move to the antecedents (Figure 9).

In the micro, meso, and macro sections, we noted that there are great differences in the antecedents mentioned in the published literature. Studies also tend to focus on a broad range of antecedents simultaneously. For instance, at the macro level, technology, financial, and political pressure are important. At the meso level, we found organizational antecedents such as culture, organizational stakeholder environments, management interventions, and technology to play a role in shaping organizational transparency. At the micro level, just three studies provided insights into the determinants of (perceived) transparency. We found, for instance, job pressures affected transparency compliance by officials and negative attitudes toward government increased transparency demand from citizens.

This heterogeneity and lack of studies at the micro level makes it harder to apply our layered framework, but it opens new avenues for future research. The vertical lines in Figure 9 present opportunities to investigate transparency dynamics from macro to micro and the other way around. First, we may investigate how specific antecedents of transparency "trickle down" from the macro to the micro level. For instance, we have seen that at the macro level, political norms and values play an important role in shaping transparency. Yet how do such political values materialize in organizational policies and culture in ministerial departments (i.e. the meso level)? Further, how does this translate into behavior of individual civil servants? Are they more willing to disclose information to stakeholders in such a culture? Many more of these trickle-down processes need to be investigated to understand how macro level "big shifts" lead to downstream changes in organizational and individual behavior.

In addition to this, and perhaps simultaneously, a process of "trickling up" is taking place. Individual changes in behavior may lead to emergent changes in the two upper levels. If grassroots organizations or individual citizens slowly start talking about government transparency, they create a demand that may lead to changes in how organizational leaders think about it, adjusting policies and strategies. Once more and more government agencies adopt this kind of transparency policy, institutional arrangements and values slowly change as well. These dynamics between agency and structure are not new to research and find a firm ground in classic works by Giddens (1984) and Ostrom (1990). Researching the trickling up and down of transparency antecedents has been done to a limited extent (e.g. Meijer 2013) but further research can really help to disentangle the short-term micro-level effects and the long-term macro-level effects on transparency.

## 7.4 Beyond Naïve Hope and Critical Cynicism: The Way Forward

The aim of this Element was to review and integrate insights from academic research on government transparency over the past few decades. We found that the big promises that transparency brought along in the first two decades of the twentieth century have not (yet) been delivered. Transparency does not automatically lead to better government performance and more trust in government. Some even consider transparency a "zombie idea": a failed policy idea that nevertheless continues to exist (Peters and Nagel 2020). Such a critical perspective on transparency fits with scholarship that emphasizes the value-laden and political nature of transparency policies. In recent years scholars have come to criticize this neutral discourse arguing that transparency is employed in strategic ways and is entangled in existing power relations (Flyverbom 2015; Wood and Aronczyk 2020).

At the same time, our extensive review of the literature highlights that transparency still is a hallmark for democratic governance and that research from all three perspectives indicates that, for instance, transparency has been relatively successful in combatting government corruption and there is some evidence that it also improves government performance. Transparency may not be the "cure-all" it once was considered to be, but is far from a "zombie idea." If this Element shows us one thing, it is that it is much easier to criticize transparency than it is to try to *understand* why transparency "works" in one context, but fails in another.

To be able to get at the success and failure we must take into account institutional and organizational contexts, and how these interact with individual behavior. Moreover, success and failure can be defined differently depending on each analytical level and so does the temporality on each level: macro studies tend to use a prolonged timeframe, whereas micro studies usually look at short-term effects. This is important in defining "success" of a transparency policy. For example, a short-term effect of a new strong transparency law may be an increase in convicted corruption cases and a subsequent lowered level of trust in government. In the long run, however, corruption cases decline and – hopefully – trust is restored (e.g. Cordis and Warren 2014). We will need much more research that "connects the dots" and provides insights into the interactions between the long and short-term effects of transparency, worldwide developments and specific instances of transparency, individual actions, and institutional transparency structures. We still believe that transparency is basically a "good idea" but we need to move beyond naïve understanding of this idea to develop notions of transparency that can really contribute to a strong democracy.

Contributing to a strong democracy is not easy in these times of contested and post-truth democracies, as we have seen in the example of the American 2020 election with which we started this Element. The role of transparency in building public trust may not be as strong as many people believed in the 1960s when FOI legislation was enacted all over the world. We should not cherish naïve hopes about the role of transparency but, at the same time, not underestimate its role in the preservation of trust in key institutions in our societies. Transparency is no miracle cure, but it remains a key component of modern democracies. Providing a sound academic understanding of this component continues to be needed as a basis for debates about the future of democracy. Academic research can lead the way to societal debates about transparency that are informed by realism rather than naïve hope or cynicism.

# References

Abushamsieh, K., López-Hernández, A. M., & Ortiz-Rodríguez, D. (2014). The development of public accounting transparency in selected Arab countries. *International Review of Administrative Sciences, 80*(2), 421–442.

Al-Aama, A. Y. (2012). E-procurement vs. online procurement: A means to increase transparency in a Saudi government organisation: The case of the Jeddah municipality. *International Journal of Procurement Management, 5*(6), 765–783.

Albu, O. B., & Flyverbom, M. (2019). Organizational transparency: Conceptualizations, conditions, and consequences. *Business & Society, 58*(2), 268–297.

Alcaraz-Quiles, F. J., Navarro-Galera, A., & Ortiz-Rodríguez, D. (2014). Factors influencing the transparency of sustainability information in regional governments: An empirical study. *Journal of Cleaner Production, 82*, 179–191.

Alcaraz-Quiles, F. J., Navarro-Galera, A., & Ortiz-Rodríguez, D. (2015). Factors determining online sustainability reporting by local governments. *International Review of Administrative Sciences, 81*(1), 79–109.

Alt, J. E., Lassen, D. D., & Rose, S. (2006). The causes of fiscal transparency: Evidence from the US states. *IMF Staff Papers, 53*(1), 30–57.

Alt, J. E., Lassen, D. D., & Skilling, D. (2002). Fiscal transparency, gubernatorial approval, and the scale of government: Evidence from the states. *State Politics & Policy Quarterly, 2*(3), 230–250.

Arapis, T., & Reitano, V. (2018). Examining the evolution of cross-national fiscal transparency. *The American Review of Public Administration, 48*(6), 550–564.

Araujo, J. F. F. E., & Tejedo-Romero, F. (2018). Does gender equality affect municipal transparency: The case of Spain. *Public Performance & Management Review, 41*(1), 69–99.

Arellano-Gault, D. (2016). Understanding the trap of systemic corruption. *Governance, 29*(4), 463–465.

Arya, O. P., & Sharma, M. S. (2014). Transparency in delivery of entitlements through empowered Civil Society Organisations (CSOs): The Consortium of Groups for Combating Corruption (CGCC) model in Rajasthan, India. *The Journal of Field Actions Science Reports, S11*, 1–8.

Avery, E. J., & Graham, M. W. (2013). Political public relations and the promotion of participatory, transparent government through social media.

*International Journal of Strategic Communication, 7*(4), 274–291. https://doi .org/10.1080/1553118X.2013.824885

Azfar, O., & Nelson, W. R. (2007). Transparency, wages, and the separation of powers: An experimental analysis of corruption. *Public Choice, 130*(3–4), 471–493.

Ball, C. (2009). What is transparency? *Public Integrity, 11*(4), 293–308.

Bastida, F., Guillamón, M. D., & Benito, B. (2017). Fiscal transparency and the cost of sovereign debt. *International Review of Administrative Sciences, 83*(1), 106–128.

Bauhr, M., Czibik, Á., de Fine Licht, J., & Fazekas, M. (2020). Lights on the shadows of public procurement: Transparency as an antidote to corruption. *Governance, 33*(3), 495–523.

Bauhr, M., & Grimes, M. (2014). Indignation or resignation: The implications of transparency for societal accountability. *Governance, 27*(2), 291–320.

Bauhr, M., & Grimes, M. (2017). Transparency to curb corruption? Concepts, measures and empirical merit. *Crime, Law and Social Change, 68*(4), 431–458.

Benito, B., & Bastida, F. (2009). Budget transparency, fiscal performance, and political turnout: An international approach. *Public Administration Review, 69*(3), 403–417.

Berliner, D. (2014). The political origins of transparency. *The Journal of Politics, 76*(2), 479–491.

Berliner, D., & Erlich, A. (2015). Competing for transparency: Political competition and institutional reform in Mexican states. *American Political Science Review, 109*(1), 110–128.

Berliner, D., Ingrams, A., & Piotrowski, S. (2018). The future of FOIA in an open government world: Implications of the open government agenda for freedom of information policy and implementation. *Villanova Law Review,* 63(December), 867–894.

Bertot, J. C., Gorham, U., Jaeger, P. T., Sarin, L. C., & Choi, H. (2014). Big data, open government and e-government: Issues, policies and recommendations. *Information Polity, 19*, 5–16.

Bertot, J. C., Jaeger, P. T., & Grimes, J. M. (2012). Promoting transparency and accountability through ICTs, social media, and collaborative e-government. *Transforming Government: People, Process and Policy, 6*(1), 78–91.

Birkinshaw, P. J. (2006). Freedom of information and openness: Fundamental human rights. *Administrative Law Review, 58*(1), 177–218.

Bolívar, M. P., del Carmen Caba Pérez, M., & López-Hernández, A. M. (2015). Online budget transparency in OECD member countries and administrative culture. *Administration & Society, 47*(8), 943–982.

Bolívar, M. P., Muñoz, L., & Hernández, A. (2013). Determinants of financial transparency in government. *International Public Management Journal, 16*(4), 557–602.

Bolívar, M. P., Pérez, C., & Hernández, A. (2007). E-government and public financial reporting: The case of Spanish regional governments. *The American Review of Public Administration, 37*(2), 142–177.

Bolman, L. G., & Deal, T. E. (2017). *Reframing organizations: Artistry, choice, and leadership* (6th ed.). San Francisco, CA: Jossey-Bass.

Bonsón, E., Torres, L., Royo, S., & Flores, F. (2012). Local e-government 2.0: Social media and corporate transparency in municipalities. *Government Information Quarterly, 29*(2), 123–132.

Bovens, M. (2007). Analysing and assessing accountability: A conceptual framework. *European Law Journal, 13*(4), 447–468. https://doi.org/10.1111/j .1468-0386.2007.00378.x

Bovens, M. (2010). Two concepts of accountability: Accountability as a virtue and as a mechanism. *West European Politics, 33*(5), 946–967.

Brusca, I., Rossi, F. M., & Aversano, N. (2016). Online sustainability information in local governments in an austerity context. *Online Information Review, 40*(4), 1–28.

Buntaine, M. T., Daniels, B., & Devlin, C. (2018). Can information outreach increase participation in community-driven development? A field experiment near Bwindi National Park, Uganda. *World Development, 106*, 407–421.

Caamaño-Alegre, J., Lago-Peñas, S., Reyes-Santias, F., & Santiago-Boubeta, A. (2013). Budget transparency in local governments: An empirical analysis. *Local Government Studies, 39*(2), 182–207.

Caba Pérez, C., Hernández, A., & Bolívar, M. (2005). Citizens' access to online governmental financial information: Practices in the European Union countries. *Government Information Quarterly, 22*(2), 258–276.

Cerrillo-i-Martínez, A. (2011). The regulation of diffusion of public sector information via electronic means: Lessons from the Spanish regulation. *Government Information Quarterly, 28*(2), 188–199.

Chen, W. Y., & Cho, F. H. T. (2019). Environmental information disclosure and societal preferences for urban river restoration: Latent class modelling of a discrete-choice experiment. *Journal of Cleaner Production, 231*, 1294–1306.

Chen, Y. (2012). A comparative study of e-government XBRL implementations: The potential of improving information transparency and efficiency. *Government Information Quarterly, 29*(4), 553–563.

Chen, Y. C., & Chang, T. W. (2020). Explaining government's online transparency on collaborative policy platforms: Risk management and configurational conditions. *Public Performance & Management Review, 43*(3), 560–586.

Chun, S. A., & Cho, J. (2012). E-participation and transparent policy decision making. *Information Polity, 17*(2), 129–145.

Cicatiello, L., De Simone, E., & Gaeta, G. L. (2018). Cross-country heterogeneity in government transparency and citizens' political efficacy: A multilevel empirical analysis. *Administration & Society, 50*(4), 595–623.

Copelovitch, M., Gandrud, C., & Hallerberg, M. (2018). Financial data transparency, international institutions, and sovereign borrowing costs. *International Studies Quarterly, 62*(1), 23–41.

Cordis, A. S., & Warren, P. L. (2014). Sunshine as disinfectant: The effect of state Freedom of Information Act laws on public corruption. *Journal of Public Economics, 115*, 18–36.

Costa, S. (2013). Do freedom of information laws decrease corruption? *The Journal of Law, Economics, & Organization, 29*(6), 1317–1343.

Cucciniello, M., & Nasi, G. (2014). Transparency for trust in government: How effective is formal transparency? *International Journal of Public Administration, 37*(13), 911–921.

Cucciniello, M., Bellè, N., Nasi, G., & Valotti, G. (2015). Assessing public preferences and the level of transparency in government using an exploratory approach. *Social Science Computer Review, 33*(5), 571–586. https://doi.org /10.1177/0894439314560849

Cucciniello, M., Nasi, G., & Valotti, G. (2012). Assessing transparency in government: Rhetoric, Reality and Desire. *45th Hawaii International Conference on System Sciences*, 2451–2461.

Cucciniello, M., Porumbescu, G. A., & Grimmelikhuijsen, S. (2017). 25 years of transparency research: Evidence and future directions. *Public Administration Review, 77*(1), 32–44.

Cuillier, D. (2016). The people's right to know: Comparing Harold L. Cross' pre-FOIA world to post-FOIA today. *Communication Law and Policy, 21*(4), 433–463.

Cuillier, D., & Piotrowski, S. J. (2009). Internet information-seeking and its relation to support for access to government records. *Government Information Quarterly, 26*(3), 441–449.

D'onza, G., Brotini, F., & Vincenzo, Z. (2017). Disclosure on measures to prevent corruption risks: A study of Italian local governments. *International Journal of Public Administration, 40*(7), 612–624. https://doi.org/10.1080/01900692 .2016.1143000

da Silva Craveiro, G., & Albano, C. (2017). Open data intermediaries: Coproduction in budget transparency. *Transforming Government: People, Process and Policy, 11*(1), 119–131.

Dahl, R. A. (2008). *Democracy and its critics*. New Haven, CT: Yale University Press.

David-Barrett, E., & Okamura, K. (2016). Norm diffusion and reputation: The rise of the extractive industries transparency initiative. *Governance, 29*(2), 227–246.

Davis, J. (1998). Access to and transmission of information: Position of the media. In V. Deckmyn and I. Thomson (Eds.), *Openness and transparency in the European Union* (pp. 121–126). Maastricht: European Institute of Public Administration.

Dawes, S. S. (2010). Stewardship and usefulness: Policy principles for information-based transparency. *Government Information Quarterly, 27*(4), 377–383.

de Boer, N. C. (2020). *On the Outside, Looking In: Understanding Transparency at the Frontline* (Doctoral dissertation, Department of Public Administration and Sociology (DPAS)).

de Boer, N., & Eshuis, J. (2018). A street-level perspective on government transparency and regulatory performance: Does relational distance matter? *Public Administration, 96*(3), 452–467.

de Boer, N., Eshuis, J., & Klijn, E. H. (2018). Does disclosure of performance information influence street-level Bureaucrats' enforcement style? *Public Administration Review, 78*(5), 694–704.

De Fine Licht, J. (2011). Do we really want to know? The potentially negative effect of transparency in decision making on perceived legitimacy. *Scandinavian Political Studies, 34*(3), 183–201.

De Fine Licht, J. (2014). Policy area as a potential moderator of transparency effects: An experiment. *Public Administration Review, 74*(3), 361–371. https://doi.org/10.1111/puar.12194

De Fine Licht, J., Naurin, D., Esaiasson, P., & Gilljam, M. (2014). When does transparency generate legitimacy? Experimenting on a context-bound relationship. *Governance, 27*(1), 111–134. https://doi.org/10.1111/gove.12021

De Graaf, G., Huberts, L., & Smulders, R. (2016). Coping with public value conflicts. *Administration & Society, 48*(9), 1101–1127.

Den Boer, M. (1998). Steamy windows: Transparency and openness in justice and home affairs. In V. Deckmyn & I. Thomson (Eds.), *Openness and transparency in the European Union* (pp. 91–105). Maastricht: European Institute of Public Administration.

Deng, S., Peng, J., & Wang, C. (2013). Fiscal transparency at the Chinese provincial level. *Public Administration, 91*(4), 947–963.

De Renzio, P., & Masud, H. (2011). Measuring and promoting budget transparency: The open budget index as a research and advocacy tool. *Governance, 24*(3), 607–616.

Deuze, M. (2002). *Journalists in The Netherlands: An analysis of the people, the issues and the (inter-)national environment.* Amsterdam, Netherlands: Aksant.

DiMaggio, P. J., & Powell, W. W. (1983). The iron cage revisited: Institutional isomorphism and collective rationality in organizational fields. *American Sociological Review, 48*(2), 147–160.

Dragos, D. C., Neamțu, B., & Cobârzan, B. V. (2012). La transparence procédurale dans les communautés rurales roumaines: le lien entre la mise en œuvre et la capacité administrative. *Revue Internationale des Sciences Administratives, 78*(1), 141–164.

Drew, C. H., & Nyerges, T. (2004). Transparency of environmental decision making: A case study of soil cleanup inside the Hanford 100 area. *Journal of Risk Research, 7*(1), 33–71. https://doi.org/10.1080/1366987042000151197

Dror, Y. (1999). Transparency and openness of quality democracy. In M. Kelly (Ed.), *Openness and transparency in governance: Challenges and opportunities* (pp. 25–43). Maastricht, The Netherlands: NISPAcee Forum.

Epley, N., & Gilovich T. (2016). The mechanics of motivated reasoning. *Journal of Economic Perspectives, 30* (3), 133–140. https://doi.org/10.1257/jep.30.3.133

Erkkilä, T. (2012). *Government transparency: Impacts and unintended consequences.* London, England: Palgrave Macmillan.

Erkkilä, T. (2020). Transparency in public administration. In William R Thompson (Ed), *Oxford Research Encyclopedia of Politics.* Oxford: Oxford University Press. https://oxfordre.com/politics/view/10.1093/acrefore/9780190228637.001.0001/acrefore-9780190228637-e-1404.

Esteller-Moré, A., & Polo Otero, J. (2012). Fiscal transparency: (Why) does your local government respond? *Public Management Review, 14*(8), 1153–1173.

Estrada, L., & Bastida, F. (2020). Effective transparency and institutional trust in Honduran municipal governments. *Administration & Society, 52*(6), 890–926. https://doi.org/10.1177/0095399719874346

Etzioni, A. (2010). Is transparency the best disinfectant. *The Journal of Political Philosophy, 18*(4), 389–404. https://doi.org/10.2139/ssrn.2731880

Eubanks, V. (2018). *Automating inequality: How high-tech tools profile, police, and punish the poor.* New York: St. Martin's Press.

Favero, N., & Bullock, J. B. (2015). How (not) to solve the problem: An evaluation of scholarly responses to common source bias. *Journal of Public Administration Research and Theory, 25*(1), 285–308.

Fenster, M. (2012). Disclosure's effects: WikiLeaks and transparency, *Iowa L. Rev.,* 97, 753.

Fenster, M. (2015). Transparency in search of a theory. *European Journal of Social Theory, 18*(2), 150–167.

Fenster, M. (2017). *The transparency fix: Secrets, leaks, and uncontrollable government information.* Stanford: Stanford University Press.

Fiol, C. M., & Lyles, M. A. (1985). Organizational learning. *The Academy of Management Review, 10*(4), 803–813.

Florini, A. (2007). *The right to know: Transparency for an open world.* New York: Columbia University Press.

Flyverbom, M. (2015). Sunlight in cyberspace? On transparency as a form of ordering. *European Journal of Social Theory, 18*(2), 168–184. https://doi.org /10.1177/1368431014555258

Fox, J. (2007). Government transparency and policymaking. *Public Choice, 131*(1/2), 23–44.

Frum D. (September 15, 2014). The transparency trap. *The Atlantic.* www .theatlantic.com/magazine/archive/2014/09/the-transparency-trap/375074/

Fukuyama, F. (2014). *Political order and political decay: From the industrial revolution to the globalization of democracy.* New York City, NY: Farrar, Straus and Giroux.

Fung, A. (2006). Varieties of participation in complex governance. *Public Administration Review, 66*(s1), 66–75.

Fung, A., Graham, M., & Weil, D. (2007). *Full disclosure: The perils and promise of transparency.* Cambridge: Cambridge University Press.

Gaines, B. J., Kuklinski, J. H., & Quirk, P. J. (2007). The logic of the survey experiment reexamined. *Political Analysis, 15*(1), 1–20.

Ganapati, S., & Reddick, C. G. (2012). Open e-government in U.S. state governments: Survey evidence from chief information officers. *Government Information Quarterly, 29*(2), 115–122.

Ganapati, S., & Reddick, C. G. (2014). The use of ICT for open government in U. S. municipalities. *Public Performance & Management Review, 37*(3), 365–387.

Gandía, J. L., Marrahí, L., & Huguet, D. (2016). Digital transparency and Web 2.0 in Spanish city councils. *Government Information Quarterly, 33*(1), 28–39.

Garde Sanchez, R., Rodríguez Bolívar, M. P., & Muñoz, L. A. (2014). Are Spanish SAIs accomplishing intosai's best practices code of transparency and accountability? *Transylvanian Review of Administrative Sciences, 10*(43), 122–145.

Garrido-Rodríguez, J. C., Zafra-Gómez, J. L., & López-Hernández, A. M. (2017). Measuring local government transparency. Influence of political sign in multidimensional analysis. *Lex Localis – Journal of Local Self-Government, 15*(4), 889–917.

Gavazza, A., & Lizzeri, A. (2009). Transparency and economic policy. *The Review of Economic Studies*, *76*(3), 1023–1048.

Giddens, A. (1984). *The constitution of society: Outline of the theory of structuration*. Berkeley: University of California Press.

Graham, F. S., Gooden, S. T., & Martin, K. J. (2016). Navigating the transparency–privacy paradox in public sector data sharing. *The American Review of Public Administration*, *46*(5), 569–591. https://doi.org/10.1177/027507401 4561116

Graham, M. (2002). *Democracy by disclosure: The rise of techno populism*. Washington, DC: Brookings Institution Press.

Grimmelikhuijsen, S. G. (2007). Transparency of government and political trust. *International Conference on Experimental Methods in Political Science*, Brussels.

Grimmelikhuijsen, S. G. (2010). Transparency of public decision-making: Towards trust in local government? *Policy & Internet*, *2*(1), 5–35. https://doi .org/10.2202/1944-2866.1024

Grimmelikhuijsen, S. G. (2011). Being transparent or spinning the message? An experiment into the effects of varying message content on trust in government. *Information Polity*, *16*(1), 35–50.

Grimmelikhuijsen, S. G. (2012). Linking transparency, knowledge, and citizen trust in government: An experiment. *International Review of Administrative Sciences*, 78(1), 50–73.

Grimmelikhuijsen, S. G., Herkes, F., Leistikow, I. et al. (2019). Can decision transparency increase citizen trust in regulatory agencies? Evidence from a representative survey experiment. *Regulation & Governance*, *15*(1), 17–31.

Grimmelikhuijsen, S. G., Jilke, S., Olsen, A. L., & Tummers, L. (2017). Behavioral public administration: Combining insights from public administration and psychology. *Public Administration Review*, *77*(1), 45–56.

Grimmelikhuijsen, S. G., & Klijn, A. (2015). The effects of judicial transparency on public trust: Evidence from a field experiment. *Public Administration*, *93*(4), 995–1011.

Grimmelikhuijsen, S. G., & Meijer, A. J. (2014). Effects of transparency on the perceived trustworthiness of a government organization: Evidence from an online experiment. *Journal of Public Administration Research and Theory*, *24*(1), 137–157. https://doi.org/10.1093/jopart/mus048

Grimmelikhuijsen, S. G., & Meijer, A. J. (2015). Does Twitter increase perceived police legitimacy? *Public Administration Review*, *75*(4), 598–607.

Grimmelikhuijsen, S. G., Piotrowski, S. J., & Van Ryzin, G. G. (2020). Latent transparency and trust in government: Unexpected findings from two survey experiments. *Government Information Quarterly*, *37*(4), 101497.

Grimmelikhuijsen, S. G., Porumbescu, G., Hong, B., & Im, T. (2013). The effect of transparency on trust in government: A cross-national comparative experiment. *Public Administration Review, 73*(4), 575–586.

Grimmelikhuijsen, S. G., & Welch, E. W. (2012). Developing and testing a theoretical framework for computer-mediated transparency of local governments. *Public Administration Review, 72*(4), 562–571.

Gunawong, P. (2015). Open government and social media: A focus on transparency. *Social Science Computer Review, 33*(5), 587–598. https://doi.org/10.1177/0894439314560685

Harrison, T., Guerrero, S., & Burke, G. (2012). Open government and e-government: Democratic challenges from a public value perspective. *Information Polity, 17*(2), 83–97.

Hazell, R., & Worthy, B. (2010). Assessing the performance of freedom of information. *Government Information Quarterly, 27*(4), 352–359.

Heald, D. (2006). Varieties of transparency. In C. Hood & D. Heald (Eds.), *Transparency: The Key to Better Governance?* (pp. 25–43). Oxford: Oxford University Press.

Heald, D. (2012). Why is transparency about public expenditure so elusive? *International Review of Administrative Sciences, 78*(1), 30–49.

Heimstädt, M., & Dobusch, L. (2018). Politics of disclosure: Organizational transparency as multiactor negotiation. *Public Administration Review, 78*(5), 727–738.

Hillebrandt, M. Z. (2017). Transparency as a platform for institutional politics: The case of the council of the European Union. *Politics and Governance, 5*(3), 62–74.

Holmberg, S., Rothstein, B., & Nasiritousi, N. (2009). Quality of government: What you get. *Annual Review of Political Science, 12*(1), 135–161.

Holmstrom, B. (1982). Moral hazard in teams. *Bell Journal of Economics, 13*(2), 324–340. https://doi.org/10.2307/3003457

Hong, H. (2014). The Internet, transparency, and government–public relationships in Seoul, South Korea. *Public Relations Review, 40*(3), 500–502.

Hood, C. (2001). Transparency. In Paul Barry Clarke and Joe Foweraker (Eds), Encyclopedia of Democratic Thought, (pp. 700–705). London: Routledge.

Hood, C. (2006). Transparency in historical perspective. In C. Hood & D. Heald (Eds.), *Transparency: The Key to Better Governance?* (pp. 4–23). Oxford: Oxford University Press.

Hood, C. (2007). What happens when transparency meets blame-avoidance? *Public Management Review, 9*(2), 191–210.

Hood, C. (2010). Accountability and transparency: Siamese twins, matching parts, awkward couple? *West European Politics*, *33*(5), 989–1009. https://doi .org/10.1080/01402382.2010.486122

Hood, C. (2011). From FOI world to WikiLeaks world: A new chapter in the transparency story. *Governance*, *24*(4), 635–638.

Hood, C., & Heald, D. (2006). *Transparency: The key to better governance?* (Vol. 135). Oxford: Oxford University Press for the British Academy.

Hyun, C., Post, A. E., & Ray, I. (2018). Frontline worker compliance with transparency reforms: Barriers posed by family and financial responsibilities. *Governance*, *31*(1), 65–83. https://doi.org/10.1111/gove .12268

Ingrams, A. (2018). Democratic transition and transparency reform. An fsQCA analysis of access to information laws in twenty-three countries. *Government Information Quarterly*, 35(3), 428–436.

Ito, T. (2002). *Is Foreign Exchange Intervention Effective? The Japanese Experiences in the 1990s.* (NBER Working Paper No. 8914). National Bureau of Economic Research. www.nber.org/papers/w8914

Janssen, M., Matheus, R., Longo, J., & Weerakkody, V. (2017). Transparency-by-design as a foundation for open government. *Transforming Government: People, Process and Policy*, *11*(*1*), 2–8.

Janssen, M., & van den Hoven, J. (2015). Big and open linked data (BOLD) in government: A challenge to transparency and privacy? *Government Information Quarterly*, *32*(4), 363–368.

Jilke, S., Olsen, A. L., Resh, W., & Siddiki, S. (2019). Microbrook, Mesobrook, Macrobrook. *Perspectives on Public Management and Governance*, *2*(4), 245–253.

John, P. (2020). Improving causal claims in public policy through randomized designs in the field. *Journal of Comparative Policy Analysis: Research and Practice*, *24*(1), 16–32.

Jordan, M., Yusuf, J., Berman, M., & Gilchrist, C. (2017). Popular financial reports as fiscal transparency mechanisms: An assessment using the fiscal transparency index for the citizen user. *International Journal of Public Administration*, *40*(8), 625–636.

Justice, J. B., Melitski, J., & Smith, D. L. (2006). E-Government as an instrument of fiscal accountability and responsiveness: Do the best practitioners employ the best practices? *The American Review of Public Administration*, *36*(3), 301–322.

Kim, C. (November 9, 2020). Poll: 70 percent of Republicans don't think the election was free and fair. *Politico*. www.politico.com/news/2020/11/09/ republicans-free-fair-elections-435488

Kim, S., & Lee, J. (2012). E-participation, transparency, and trust in local government. *Public Administration Review, 72*(6), 819–828.

Kimball, M. B. (2011). Mandated state-level open government training programs. *Government Information Quarterly, 28*(4), 474–483.

Kosack, S., & Fung, A. (2014). Does transparency improve governance? *Annual Review of Political Science, 17*(1), 65–87. https://doi.org/10.1146/annurev-polisci-032210-144356

Kozlowski, S. W. J., & Klein, K. J. (2000). A multilevel approach to theory and research in organizations: Contextual, temporal, and emergent processes. In K. J. Klein & S. W. J. Kozlowski (Eds.), *Multilevel Theory, Research, and Methods in Organizations: Foundations, Extensions, and New Directions* (pp. 3–90). San Francisco: Jossey-Bass.

Lagunes, P., & Pocasangre, O. (2019). Dynamic transparency: An audit of Mexico's freedom of information act. *Public Administration, 97*(1), 162–176.

Larbi, B., Baiden, B. K., & Agyekum, K. (2019). Compliance with transparency provisions in the public procurement act, 2003 (Act 663). *International Journal of Procurement Management, 12*(1), 112–133.

Lerner, J., & Tetlock, P. E. (1999). Accounting for the effects of accountability. *Psychological Bulletin, 125*(2), 255–275.

Li, G., Yefen, C., & Zhong, F. (2019). Pollution transparency mechanisms for commodities: A game-theoretic analysis. *Journal of Cleaner Production, 237*(10), 117789.

Lindstedt, C., & Naurin, D. (2010). Transparency is not enough: Making transparency effective in reducing corruption. *International Political Science Review, 31*(3), 301–322. https://doi.org/10.1177/0192512110377602

Liu, A. C. (2016). Two faces of transparency: The regulations of people's republic of china on open government information. *International Journal of Public Administration, 39*(6), 492–503.

Lourenço, R. P. (2015). An analysis of open government portals: A perspective of transparency for accountability. *Government Information Quarterly, 32*(3), 323–332.

Mason, D., Hillenbrand, C., & Money, K. (2014). Are informed citizens more trusting? Transparency of performance data and trust towards a British police force. *Journal of Business Ethics, 122*(2), 321–341.

McDermott, P. (2010). Building open government. *Government Information Quarterly, 27*(4), 401–413.

Meijer, A. (2015). Government transparency in historical perspective: From the ancient regime to open data in the Netherlands. *International Journal of Public Administration, 38*(3), 189–199.

Meijer, A. J. (2000). Anticipating accountability processes. *Archives and Manuscripts*, *28*(1), 52–63.

Meijer, A. J. (2003). Transparent government: Parliamentary and legal accountability in an information age. *Information Polity*, *8*(1/2), 67–78.

Meijer, A. J. (2005). Risk maps on the internet: Transparency and the management of risks. *Information Polity*, *10*(1), 105–113.

Meijer, A. J. (2007). Publishing public performance results on the internet: Do stakeholders use the internet to hold Dutch public service organizations to account? *Government Information Quarterly*, *24*(1), 165–185.

Meijer, A. J. (2009a). Does transparency lead to better education? The effects in the Netherlands of publishing school performance indicators on the internet. In A. Meijer, K. Boersma & P. Wagenaar (Eds.), *ICTs, Citizens & Governance: After the Hype!* (pp. 38–49). Amsterdam: IOS Press.

Meijer, A. J. (2009b). Understanding modern transparency. *International Review of the Administrative Sciences*, *75*(2), 255–269.

Meijer, A. J. (2013). Understanding the complex dynamics of transparency. *Public Administration Review*, *73*(3), 429–439. https://doi.org/10.1111/puar.12032

Meijer, A. J., & Homburg, V. (2009). Disclosure and compliance: The "pillory" as an innovative regulatory instrument. *Information Polity*, *14*(4), 263–278.

Meijer, A. J., 't Hart, P., & Worthy, B. (2018). Accessing government transparency: An interpretative framework. *Administration and Society*, *50*(4), 501–526. https://doi.org/10.1177%2F0095399715598341

Meijer, R., Conradie, P., & Choenni, S. (2014). Reconciling Contradictions of Open Data Regarding Transparency, Privacy, Security and Trust. *Journal of Theoretical and Applied Electronic Commerce Research*, *9*(3), 32-44.

Michael, B., & Bates, M. (2003). Assessing international fiscal and monetary transparency: The role of standards, knowledge management and project design. *International Public Management Journal*, *6*(2), 95–116.

Michener, G. (2011). FOI laws around the world. *Journal of Democracy*, *22*(2), 145–159.

Michener, G. (2015). How cabinet size and legislative control shape the strength of transparency laws. *Governance*, *28*(1), 77–94.

Michener, G. (2019). Gauging the impact of transparency policies. *Public Administration Review*, *79*(1), 136–139.

Michener, G., & Bersch, K. (2013). Identifying transparency. *Information Polity*, *18*(3), 233–242.

Michener, G., Coelho, J., & Moreira, D. (2021). Are governments complying with transparency? Findings from 15 years of evaluation. *Government Information Quarterly*, *38*(2), 101565.

Michener, G., & Ritter, O. (2017). Comparing resistance to open data performance measurement: Public education in Brazil and the UK. *Public Administration, 95*(1), 4–21.

Michener, G., & Worthy, B. (2018). The information-gathering matrix: A framework for conceptualizing the use of freedom of information laws. *Administration & Society, 50*(4), 476–500.

Moynihan. D. (2018). A great schism approaching? Towards a micro and macro public administration. *Journal of Behavioral Public Administration, 1*(1), https://doi.org/10.30636/jbpa.11.15

Navarro-Galera, A., Alcaraz-Quiles, F. J., & Ortiz-Rodríguez, D. (2016). Online dissemination of information on sustainability in regional governments: Effects of technological factors. *Government Information Quarterly, 33*(1), 53–66.

Navarro-Galera, A., Ruiz-Lozano, M., Tirado-Valencia, P., & Ríos-Berjillos, A. D. L. (2017). Promoting sustainability transparency in European local governments: An empirical analysis based on administrative cultures. *Sustainability, 9*(3), 432.

North, D. C. (1991). Institutions. *Journal of Economic Perspectives, 5*(1), 97–112.

Obama, B. (January 21, 2009). Memorandum for the heads of executive departments and agencies: Transparency and open government. [Memorandum]. *Federal Register.* www.whitehouse.gov/the_press_office/TransparencyandOpenGovernment

Ortiz-Rodríguez, D., Navarro-Galera, A., & Alcaraz-Quiles, F. J. (2018). The influence of administrative culture on sustainability transparency in European local governments. *Administration & Society, 50*(4), 555–594.

Ostrom, E. (1990). Governing the commons: The evolution of institutions for collective action. Cambridge: Cambridge University Press.

Overman, S., & Schillemans, T. (2022). Toward a public administration theory of felt accountability. *Public Administration Review, 82*(1), 12–22, https://doi.org/10.1111/puar.13417

Park, H., & Blenkinsopp, J. (2011). The roles of transparency and trust in the relationship between corruption and citizen satisfaction. *International Review of Administrative Sciences, 77*(2), 254–274.

Park, H., & Blenkinsopp, J. (2017). Transparency is in the eye of the beholder: The effects of identity and negative perceptions on ratings of transparency via surveys. *International Review of Administrative Sciences, 83* (1_suppl), 177–194.

Peisakhin, L. (2011). Transparency and corruption: Evidence from India. *The Journal of Law and Economics, 55*(1), 129–149.

Peters, B., & Nagel, M. (2020). *Zombie ideas: Why failed policy ideas persist* (Elements in public policy). Cambridge: Cambridge University Press.

Pina, V., & Torres, L. (2019). Online transparency and corporate governance in Spanish governmental agencies. *Online Information Review, 43*(4), 653–675.

Pina, V., Torres, L., & Royo, S. (2010). Is e-government leading to more accountable and transparent local governments? An overall view. *Financial Accountability & Management, 26*(1), 3–20.

Piotrowski, S. J. (2007). *Governmental transparency in the path of administrative reform.* Albany, NY: State University of New York Press.

Piotrowski, S. J. (2017). The "open government reform" movement: The case of the open government partnership and US transparency policies. *The American Review of Public Administration, 47*(2), 155–171. https://doi.org /10.1177%2F0275074016676575

Piotrowski, S. J., & Borry, E. (2010). An analytic framework for open meetings and transparency. *Public Administration & Management, 15*(1), 138–176.

Piotrowski, S. J., & Rosenbloom, D. H. (2002). Nonmission–based values in results–oriented public management: The case of freedom of information. *Public Administration Review, 62,* 643–657.

Piotrowski, S. J., Grimmelikhuijsen, S., & Deat, F. (2019). Numbers over narratives? How government message strategies affect citizens' attitudes. *Public Performance & Management Review, 42*(5), 1005–1028. https://doi .org/10.1080/15309576.2017.1400992

Piotrowski, S. J., & Van Ryzin, G. G. (2007). Citizen attitudes toward transparency in local government. *The American Review of Public Administration, 37*(3), 306–323. https://doi.org/10.1177/0275074006296777

Pollitt, C., & Bouckaert, G. (2004). *Public management reform: A comparative analysis.* (2nd ed.). New York: Oxford University Press.

Popper, K. (1945). *The open society and its enemies.* London: Routledge.

Porumbescu, G. (2015). Using transparency to enhance responsiveness and trust in local government: Can it work? *State and Local Government Review, 47*(3), 205–213.

Porumbescu, G., & Grimmelikhuijsen, S. (2018). Linking decision-making procedures to decision acceptance and citizen voice: Evidence from two studies. *The American Review of Public Administration, 48*(8), 902–914. https://doi.org/10.1177/0275074017734642

Porumbescu, G., Bellé, N., Cucciniello, M., & Nasi, G. (2017). Translating policy transparency into policy understanding and policy support: Evidence from a survey experiment. *Public Administration, 95*(4), 990–1008.

Porumbescu, G. A. (2017). Does transparency improve citizens' perceptions of government performance? Evidence from Seoul, South Korea. *Administration & Society*, *49*(3), 443–468.

Porumbescu, G. A. (2018). Assessing the implications of online mass media for citizens' evaluations of government. *Policy Design and Practice*, *1*(3), 233–240.

Porumbescu, G. A., & Im, T. (2015). Using transparency to reinforce responsibility and responsiveness. In J. Perry & R. Christensen, (Eds.), *The Handbook of public administration*, (3rd ed.) (pp. 120–136). San Francisco, CA: John Wiley.

Porumbescu, G. A., Cucciniello, M., Belle, N., & Nasi, G. (2020). Only hearing what they want to hear: Assessing when and why performance information triggers intentions to coproduce. *Public Administration*, 99(4) 789–802. https://doi.org/10.1111/padm.12697

Porumbescu, G. A., Grimes, M., & Grimmelikhuijsen, S. (2021). Capturing the social relevance of government transparency and accountability using a behavioral lens. *Journal of Behavioral Public Administration*, *4*(1), 1–8. https://doi.org/10.30636/jbpa.41.241

Porumbescu, G. A., Lindeman, M. I., Ceka, E., & Cucciniello, M. (2017). Can transparency foster more understanding and compliant citizens? *Public Administration Review*, *77*(6), 840–850.

Pozen, D. E. (2018). Transparency's ideological drift. *Yale Law Journal*, *128*, 100–165.

Pozen, D. E. (2019). Hardball and/as anti-hardball. *N.Y.U. Journal of Legislation & Public Policy*, *21*, 949–955.

Pozen, D. E. (2020). Seeing transparency more clearly. *Public Administration Review*, *80*(2), 326–331.

Puron-Cid, G. (2014). Factors for a successful adoption of budgetary transparency innovations: A questionnaire report of an open government initiative in Mexico. *Government Information Quarterly*, *31*(1), S49–S62.

Rauh, C. (2016). *A responsive technocracy? EU politicisation and the consumer policies of the European commission*. Colchester: ECPR Press.

Relly, J. E., & Cuillier, D. (2010). A comparison of political, cultural, and economic indicators of access to information in Arab and non-Arab states. *Government Information Quarterly*, *27*(4), 360–370.

Ríos, A. M., Benito, B., & Bastida, F. (2013). Determinants of central government budget disclosure: An international comparative analysis. *Journal of Comparative Policy Analysis: Research and Practice*, *15*(3), 235–254.

Roberts, A. (2000). Less government, more secrecy: Reinvention and the weakening of freedom of information law. *Public Administration Review*, *60*(4), 308–320.

Roberts, A. (2006). *Blacked out: Government secrecy in the information age.* Cambridge: Cambridge University Press.

Roberts, A. (2012). Wikileaks: The illusion of transparency. *International Review of the Administrative Sciences, 78*(1), 116–133.

Roberts, A. (2020). Bridging levels of public administration: How macro shapes meso and micro. *Administration & Society, 52*(4), 631–656.

Roberts, A. S. (2005). Spin control and freedom of information: Lessons for the United Kingdom from Canada. *Public Administration, 83*(1), 1–23.

Roberts, J. (2009). No one is perfect: The limits of transparency and ethic for "intelligent" accountability. *Accountability, Organization and Society, 34*(8), 957–970.

Rodríguez Bolívar, M. P., del Carmen Caba Pérez, M., & López-Hernández, A. M. (2015). Online budget transparency in OECD member countries and administrative culture. *Administration & Society, 47*(8), 943–982.

Roelofs, P. (2019). Transparency and mistrust: Who or what should be made transparent? *Governance, 32*(3), 565–580.

Rose, S., & Smith, D. (2012). Budget slack, institutions, and transparency. *Public Administration Review, 72*(2), 187–195.

Royo, S., Yetano, A., & Acerete, B. (2014). E-participation and environmental protection: Are local governments really committed? *Public Administration Review, 74*(1), 87–98.

Ruijer, H. J. M. (2013). Proactive transparency and government communication in the USA and the Netherlands (Dissertation). https://www.proquest.com/docview/1500831668?pq-origsite=gscholar&fromopenview=true

Ruijer, H. E. (2013). Proactive transparency and government communication in the USA and the Netherlands. Virginia Commonwealth University.

Ruijer, E. (2017). Proactive transparency in the United States and the Netherlands: The role of government communication officials. *The American Review of Public Administration, 47*(3), 354–375.

Ruijer, E., & Meijer, A. (2016). National transparency regimes: Rules or principles? A comparative analysis of the United States and The Netherlands. *International Journal of Public Administration, 39*(11), 895–908.

Ruijer, E., Détienne, F., Baker, M., Groff, J., & Meijer, A. (2020). The politics of open government data: Understanding organizational responses to pressure for more transparency. *The American Review of Public Administration, 50*(3), 260–274.

Safarov, I. (2019). Institutional dimensions of open government data implementation: Evidence from the Netherlands, Sweden, and the UK. *Public performance & management review, 42*(2), 305–328.

Scholtes, E. (2012). Transparantie, icoon van een dolende overheid. Den Haag: Boom Lemma.

Schudson, M. (2020). The shortcomings of transparency for democracy. *American Behavioral Scientist, 64*(11), 1670–1678.

Scott, P. G., & Falcone, S. (1998). Comparing public and private organizations: An exploratory analysis of three frameworks. *The American Review of Public Administration, 28*(2), 126–145.

Searson, E. M., & Johnson, M. A. (2010). Transparency laws and interactive public relations: An analysis of Latin American government Web sites. *Public Relations Review, 36*(2), 120–126.

Simon, H. A. (1947a). *Administrative behavior: A study of decision-making processes in administrative organization.* New York: Macmillan.

Simon, H. A. (1947b). A comment on "the science of public administration." *Public Administration Review, 7*(3), 200–203.

Skyttner, L. (2005). *General systems theory: Problems, perspectives, practice.* Singapore: World Scientific.

Song, C., & Lee, J. (2016). Citizens' use of social media in government, perceived transparency, and trust in government. *Public Performance & Management Review, 39*(2), 430–453.

Spicer, Z. (2017). Bridging the accountability and transparency gap in inter-municipal collaboration. *Local Government Studies, 43*(3), 388–407.

Stewart, D. R. C., & Davis, C. N. (2016). Bringing back full disclosure: A call for dismantling FOIA. *Communication Law and Policy, 21*(4), 515–537.

Szabo, S., Profiroiu, M., Porumbescu, G. A., & Ceka, E. (2016). Linking objective-oriented transparency to political leadership and strategic planning. *Transylvanian Review of Administrative Sciences, 12*, 75–90.

*The Right to Info.* (n.d.). Access to information laws: Overview and statutory goals. www.right2info.org/access-to-information-laws

Thornton, J. B., & Thornton, E. (2013). Assessing state government financial transparency websites. *Reference Services Review, 41*(2), 366–387.

Van Erp, J. (2011). Naming without shaming: The publication of sanctions in the Dutch financial market. *Regulation & Governance, 5*(3), 287–308. https://doi.org/10.1111/j.1748-5991.2011.01115.x

Van Zyl, A. (2014). How civil society organizations close the gap between transparency and accountability. *Governance, 27*(2), 347–356.

Weiss, T. G. (2000). Governance, good governance and global governance: Conceptual and actual challenges. *Third World Quarterly, 21*(5), 795–814.

Welch, E. W., & Wong, W. (2001). Global information technology pressure and government accountability: The mediating effect of domestic context on web site openness. *Journal of Public Administration Research & Theory, 11*(4), 509–538.

Welch, E. W., Hinnant, C. C., & Moon, M. J. (2005). Linking citizen satisfaction with e-government and trust in government. *Journal of Public Administration Research and Theory, 15*(3), 371–391.

Westerback, L. K. (2000). Toward best practices for strategic information technology management. *Government Information Quarterly, 17*(1), 27–41.

Wilson, B., & Chakraborty, A. (2019). Planning smart(er) cities: The promise of civic technology. *Journal of Urban Technology, 26*(4), 29–51.

Wood, T., & Aronczyk, M. (2020). Publicity and transparency. *American Behavioral Scientist, 64*(11), 1531–1544.

Worthy, B. (2010). More open but not more trusted? The effect of the freedom of information act 2000 on the United Kingdom central government. *Governance, 23*(4), 561–582.

Worthy, B. (2013). "Some are more open than others": Comparing the impact of the Freedom of Information act 2000 on local and central government in the UK. *Journal of Comparative Policy Analysis: Research and Practice, 15*(5), 395–414.

Worthy, B. (2015). The impact of open data in the UK: Complex, unpredictable and political. *Public Administration, 93*(3), 788–805.

Worthy, B., John, P., & Vannoni, M. (2017). Transparency at the parish pump: A field experiment to measure the effectiveness of freedom of information requests in England. *Journal of Public Administration Research and Theory, 27*(3), 485–500.

Wu, W., Ma, L., & Yu, W. (2017). Government transparency and perceived social equity: Assessing the moderating effect of citizen trust in China. *Administration & Society, 49*(6), 882–906.

Xiao, W. (2010). China's limited push model of FOI legislation. *Government Information Quarterly, 27*(4), 346–351.

Yavuz, N., & Welch, E. (2014). Factors affecting openness of local government websites: Examining the differences across planning, finance and police departments. *Government Information Quarterly, 31*(4), 574–583.

Yu-Che, C. (2012). A comparative study of e-government XBRL implementations: The potential of improving information transparency and efficiency. *Government Information Quarterly, 29*(4), 553–563.

Zakaria, F., & Yew, L. (1994). Culture is destiny: A conversation with Lee Kuan Yew. *Foreign Affairs, 73*(2), 109–126. https://doi.org/10.2307/20045923

Zuo, A., & Wheeler, S. (2019). Maximising the use of national pollution data: Views from stakeholders in Australia. *Journal of Cleaner Production,* 455–463. https://doi.org/10.1016/j.jclepro.2019.03.029

# Acknowledgments

Each author contributed equally to this Element. The authors would like to acknowledge the valuable input and feedback they have received from their colleagues, in particular Esther Nieuwenhuizen and Alasdair Roberts. Also they thank the reviewers for their thorough and helpful feedback on the manuscript, the pleasant and diligent editorial support from Cambridge University Press, and they are grateful for the support from their family and friends through the process of preparing this manuscript.

# Cambridge Elements

# Public Policy

## M. Ramesh
*National University of Singapore (NUS)*

M. Ramesh is UNESCO Chair on Social Policy Design at the Lee Kuan Yew School of Public Policy, NUS. His research focuses on governance and social policy in East and Southeast Asia, in addition to public policy institutions and processes. He has published extensively in reputed international journals. He is Co-editor of Policy and Society and Policy Design and Practice.

## Michael Howlett
*Simon Fraser University, British Columbia*

Michael Howlett is Burnaby Mountain Professor and Canada Research Chair (Tier 1) in the Department of Political Science, Simon Fraser University. He specialises in public policy analysis, and resource and environmental policy. He is currently editor-in-chief of Policy Sciences and co-editor of the Journal of Comparative Policy Analysis, Policy and Society and Policy Design and Practice.

## Xun WU
*Hong Kong University of Science and Technology*

Xun WU is Professor and Head of the Division of Public Policy at the Hong Kong University of Science and Technology. He is a policy scientist whose research interests include policy innovations, water resource management and health policy reform. He has been involved extensively in consultancy and executive education, his work involving consultations for the World Bank and UNEP.

## Judith Clifton
*University of Cantabria*

Judith Clifton is Professor of Economics at the University of Cantabria, Spain. She has published in leading policy journals and is editor-in-chief of the Journal of Economic Policy Reform. Most recently, her research enquires how emerging technologies can transform public administration, a forward-looking cutting-edge project which received €3.5 million funding from the Horizon2020 programme.

## Eduardo Araral
*National University of Singapore (NUS)*

Eduardo Araral is widely published in various journals and books and has presented in forty conferences. He is currently Co-Director of the Institute of Water Policy at the Lee Kuan Yew School of Public Policy, NUS, and is a member of the editorial board of Journal of Public Administration Research and Theory and the board of the Public Management Research Association.

## About the Series

Elements in Public Policy is a concise and authoritative collection of assessments of the state of the art and future research directions in public policy research, as well as substantive new research on key topics. Edited by leading scholars in the field, the series is an ideal medium for reflecting on and advancing the understanding of critical issues in the public sphere. Collectively, it provides a forum for broad and diverse coverage of all major topics in the field while integrating different disciplinary and methodological approaches.

**Cambridge Elements** ☰

# Public Policy

---

## Elements in the Series

*Policy Entrepreneurs and Dynamic Change*
Michael Mintrom

*Making Global Policy*
Diane Stone

*Understanding and Analyzing Public Policy Design*
Saba Siddiki

*Zombie Ideas: Why Failed Policy Ideas Persist*
Brainard Guy Peters and Maximilian Lennart Nagel

*Defining Policy Analysis: A Journey that Never Ends*
Beryl A. Radin

*Integrating Logics in the Governance of Emerging Technologies: The Case of Nanotechnology*l
Derrick Mason Anderson and Andrew Whitford

*Truth and Post-Truth in Public Policy*
Frank Fischer

*Disrupted Governance: Towards a New Policy Science*
Kris Hartley Glen David Kuecker

*Digital Technology, Politics, and Policy-Making*
Fabrizio Gilardi

*Public Policy and Universities: The Interplay of Knowledge and Power*
Andrew Gunn and Michael Mintrom

*Government Transparency: State of the Art and New Perspectives*
Gregory Porumbescu, Albert Meijer, and Stephan Grimmelikhuijsen

A full series listing is available at: www.cambridge.org/EPPO

Printed in the United States
by Baker & Taylor Publisher Services